Lark Ascending

Roy W Taylor

First published 2010 by
Bob Anthony Book Ltd.
28 Nicholls Court
Thorplands
Northampton
NN3 8AP
story.joe@gmail.com

For Memories Are made Of This

For my two wonderful sons
Andrew and Chris

Contents

AN ISLAND PRELUDE

At low tide on Strangford Lough, it is perfectly possible to walk along the narrow causeway to Rough Island. On this April day, Eileen and I are taking a walk round the island with our friends, Mel and Carolyn, who would often stay with us on their visits to Northern Ireland. They are keen bird watchers, and their expert knowledge makes up for our own woeful ignorance.

At this time of day the tide is out, but there are a few residual pools which attract such birds as brent geese, oystercatchers and turnstones. We peer at them with binoculars from time to time.

We have almost done a circuit of the island when something unusual takes place. A bird alights on a branch close to where we are standing, and remains there for almost a minute while we watch. The bird is a skylark. In our Devon days, when Eileen and I walked the South West Coast Path, we would sometimes hear the call of a cuckoo or the sweet singing of a skylark high above us, but we did not catch sight of them. The sighting on this occasion we regard as a love-gift to us from the Lord. We hardly dare to move, lest we should disturb it.

All too soon, the skylark has flown away, and we continue our walk; but our hearts are warmed through this encounter.

The events of this book begin a year and a quarter later.

1
WEDDINGS MAKE YOU TIRED

If you have sons rather than daughters, weddings should be easy. Traditionally, it is the bride's parents who bear the main responsibility for the wedding and the reception. However, we had to be different. Our younger son, Chris, had already married an Argentinian girl. Now it was the turn of his brother Andrew to marry a girl from South Korea. Whatever happened to the girl next door? In both cases, the main responsibility for the arrangements fell to us.

The preparations were not without stress. Entertaining wedding guests usually involves a lot of catering, and our 'fridge had broken down. A succession of repair men came to the house, each of them promising success, but failing to deliver. In the end, we had to make use of various friends' refrigerators to store the Irish Stew and other foodstuffs. The situation was not remedied until several weeks after the wedding, when we were allowed to acquire a replacement. By then, of course, the pressure was off.

The next problem was to accommodate all the guests, as many had travelled great distances. This was mainly Eileen's responsibility. Many of the Koreans chose to stay at the second home of Eileen's sister, Betty, just down the road from us. How they all found a place to sleep remains a mystery. They liked the seaside views, and later, after she had visited some of the tourist spots in London, the bride's mother was heard to say: "I much prefer Ireland". Others were placed in B&Bs and private houses. As for me, I was the transport officer: it was my task to ensure that people got safely from one venue to another. Eileen also took it upon herself to arrange a ceilidh (a sort of Irish party that would begin with a display of Irish dancing) for the evening. All this involved plenty of preparation.

We decided to hold the ceremony at St. Saviour's, Greyabbey, as I was ministering there during a vacancy. The people of that church were delighted that we had made this choice, and did everything they could to ensure that the occasion was a success.

"A horrible day for a wedding!" remarked the taxi driver as he took Eileen that morning through driving rain to the hairdresser's appointment in Donaghadee. It was more like November than August. However, at the start of the afternoon it became warm, dry and sunny, and stayed that way until the service and the photographs were over. So even the weather was under God's control. Had the weather remained poor, the Korean bridesmaids, in their short off-the-shoulder dresses would have been very uncomfortable.

The service was attended not only by the invited guests, but also by familiar church members. When the bride's mother arrived in traditional costume, and I escorted her to her place, there was a ripple of interest. Eileen, looking radiant in her new cerise dress, read from 1 Corinthians 13. It was, of course, a passage about love, but it also contained the words: "Now we see but a poor reflection, then we shall see face to face. Now I know in part; then I shall know fully, even as I am fully known." We did not know at the time that those words would soon take on a much deeper significance. I preached with great freedom on the subject of 'love'. Many people remarked on the tangible sense of the Lord's presence during the whole service. He bathed us all in his love on that special day.

For the photographs we had the use of the old abbey ruins, which formed a romantic backdrop. Andrew and Jmin had asked a Korean from London to take the photographs. As he had never done wedding photography before, he needed a lot of guidance. He insisted also on working all the time with his trilby on.

The reception took place in the church's new hall, a converted portakabin. The décor would not have disgraced a top class hotel and the food, prepared by professional caterers, was excellent. The evening ceilidh was also a great success. The Greyabbey people kindly provided an evening buffet without cost.

We both shared the task of getting guests back to airports. At last the excitement was over, and we could return to normal life. Eileen was feeling very tired, but, recalling her experience of the earlier wedding several years before, she supposed it would gradually wear off.

In her occasional diary, she wrote of that day:
> *"What a wedding day. I learnt so much. God's presence was so real. You could sense his joy in our joy. So much reconciliation – hugs all round.... Iris wrote to us afterwards and made the comment that 'love was everywhere'. The whole occasion was just so happy."*

> *"I told Andrew, as I dropped them off at the airport, that I was just so proud of him. He did look so fabulous in his gorgeous hand made suit."*

*

A week later, we drove to the Christian Renewal Centre at Rostrevor, near the border. Our links with the centre went back to 1976, when it was an important place for reconciliation at the height of the 'troubles'. Now it had become a house of prayer. The community had become very small, and they relied on voluntary helpers, who would come for short periods to assist them in such duties as serving food, washing up, cleaning bathrooms, ironing bed linen and so on. We would offer our help from time to time, and would in turn benefit from the good Christian fellowship which we enjoyed there. We were also blessed by some of the people we met. At times there would be groups of reformed drug addicts, mainly from Dublin. One lad was heard to remark: "It's f--- wonderful to be a Christian".

The workload on this occasion was not heavy, and we were able to rest on our bed after lunch and go for short afternoon walks. One morning Eileen, feeling low, found it was only with great effort that she could get down to breakfast. It did not help that she had never been a morning person. For the most part, however, we were both able to perform our duties as normal.

I returned home on the Saturday afternoon, as I had services to conduct on Sunday. While I was away, two members of the community, together with some Catholic charismatics and Eileen, prayed together for a Catholic women in her 40s who was sick. This is how a member of the community describes it:

> *"When B.... arrived she looked very poorly but was very open to receive prayer. The prayer time was led by Eugene Boyle, but almost everyone joined in, and there was a very wonderful sense of Jesus' presence. It was as though he was walking through the room. I have rarely felt anything like it. There was such a sense of his love and peace in our midst – it was palpable. B--- didn't ask us to pray for her healing but that God would be with her family through whatever happened. I seem to remember that Eileen prayed about the love of God, but I can't remember very clearly. I do remember talking to her afterwards and her commenting on how present Jesus had been, and how good it was to pray with these lovely Catholics."*

> *"D... and her sister B... were very moved by the sense of God's love for them, and after a short time went on to the Monastery for more prayer. It later transpired that B..., from that time on, was very much*

11

at peace and confessed that she felt very close to God and had never been happier in her life. D..., though upset at the later loss of her sister, also felt the love of God with her, and she is coming to terms with the death of her much beloved sister."

The same friend said that Eileen was an important contributer to this process.

*

On Saturday we went on a National Trust outing for which we had booked some time previously. The plan was to make the ascent of a mountain called Slieve Donard. We all met up at a car park in Newcastle, County Down, from which we were taken to our starting point in a beat-up landrover. Our leader was an enthusiast called David, whose love of the Mournes had led him to move across permanently from his native Newcastle-upon-Tyne. He was one of a growing number of English folk, who have taken advantage of the more peaceful conditions to make their home in the province.

We began by tracing our way through a boulder-strewn area, adjacent to a forest. A little further on, we came to a place where stones had been fitted together to make an artificial path, a process which, David informed us, involved great expense. In due course a light mist descended, making it damp and cool, and many of us were glad that we had brought waterproofs. Often we had to stop to let stragglers catch up.

After crossing a stream, we made a steeper ascent up to a place called The Saddle, where a wall afforded some shelter, and here we ate our packed lunch. I was surprised to see how many other walkers there were, some of them too lightly dressed for the conditions. There were also some fell runners, whose energy seemed boundless and challenging.

Eileen and I both loved the great outdoors. Those holidays that we spent walking the South West Coast Path were some of the best times of our life. Veterans as we were, the completion of this ascent should have been no problem; but when David gave us a choice of going up or down, Eileen asked: "Do you mind if we go down?" I chose to go down with her, and so did a few others. Since weather conditions had worsened, I did not regret the choice. We enjoyed a cup of tea at the Mourne Cafe before driving home, both of us unaware at the time that this would be our last long walk together.

*

12

Throughout our married life, we tried to make our home a warm and hospitable place. In our last parish, in North Devon, it was hard to get people to attend Bible Studies, but they were happy to come to dinner parties. In our retirement we still enjoyed giving hospitality.

Ian Smith had recently moved across from York to head up the work of the Church Mission Society in Ireland. We wrote to welcome him, and then met up with him. To our surprise, we found that I had known his wife, Carol. When her father became vicar at my home church in Blackpool, I had run a children's club, of which Carol and her brother Kevin were keen members; and both claimed to have been helped by it. I had not seen Carol for several decades. It seemed a good idea to invite the couple over for a meal. This we did on 8 September. It was a happy occasion, with plenty of good conversation.

What we did not know then was that, within a very short period of time, both Ian and Eileen would be suffering from terminal illness.

*

Eileen had been trained at the Faith Mission Bible College in Edinburgh. As a missionary in Taiwan, she was free to teach Bible as she had opportunity. When we returned to England, she found herself in the unaccustomed role of minister's wife. I was the one with the upfront role of preaching and teaching. Eileen had the gifts and the experience, but, since her training was not recognized by the Anglican Church, she would not be allowed to teach publicly without being trained all over again. This was not something she was prepared to do.

However, at this stage, opportunities for ministry were growing. Every Easter the Belfast Chinese Church holds a retreat at Castlewellan. The old castle building is usually thronged with Chinese, all anxious to learn more about their faith, and maybe also excited about living in a castle! This year Eileen and I were the main speakers in the English section. We both gave talks, and these were much appreciated.

Now, in September, there were further opportunities for ministry. As head of the parish's mission committee, Eileen was invited on Mission Sunday to conduct services and speak at both our local churches in Millisle and Carrowdore. Her gifts were being recognized at last.

We had both been involved in an Alpha course at Kircubbin that included both Roman Catholics and Anglicans. This September we began follow-up meetings in Greyabbey, and Eileen and I both led discussion groups.

There was also further ministry at the Chinese Church. We gave a course on 'Christian Living'. I preached the first time and Eileen the other two times on three successive Sundays. We were both delighted that such opportunities had opened up for us.

*

When revival had hit Northern Ireland in the past, it had always failed to reach the Ards Peninsula, and we had long been concerned about this.

In June of this year we had visited St. Andrew's Chorleywood, a strongly charismatic Anglican Church to the north of London. During the worship, there was special prayer for Northern Ireland and for our peninsula in particular. Those of us with Irish connections were invited to the front to represent the rest, and much fervent prayer was offered. Eileen wrote:

> *"I felt a real burden to pray for the Ards Peninsula which the Lord cut across and said that through the praise, he had broken the spirit of death through the peninsula. We were to go back and declare this and start a Peninsula Praise."*

I talked with two of our local ministers, one Presbyterian and the other Methodist, to share this vision, and each of them said separately, "God has already been leading me toward this". It might have seemed inappropriate for a retired couple to spearhead such an initiative, but now local serving clergy had taken the burden of responsibility upon themselves. We were free to sit back and watch God acting through others. Eileen and I went to see our Bishop, and he readily expressed his support for the project.

*

Four years earlier, Eileen had had a malignant melanoma removed from her jaw during a visit to Australia. This was followed by regular check-ups. On 16 September she had a last appointment with the oncologist. "Good news," she was told. "You are in the clear, there is no further sign of the cancer, and you will not need any more appointments."

14

This was ironic, for Eileen was still feeling very tired. In fact, the tiredness was increasing: it appeared to be something more than reaction to the wedding. She went to see her GP and an appointment was arranged at the Ards Community Hospital for an investigation in October.

On 19 September, Eileen wrote:

> *"I have struggled physically with exhaustion since the wedding. It is hard sometimes to separate what is physical and what is spiritual attack.*
>
> *Talking to Joy, she shared what God had been saying to her: 'What is your heart's desire? Go for that in prayer – big prayers.'*
>
> *My heart's desire -*
> * *to be the woman God created me to be;*
> * *to walk tall in this knowledge;*
> * *to be filled with His love and His joy;*
> * *to share the joy of God's love with others;*
> * *for complete 'well-being' (Exodus 20:24 NRSV).*
>
> *This is God's truth. Satan's lie is that I have come to the end of my period of 'well-being' and it is a slide downhill to the grave.*
>
> *No way!"*

This was her final entry. It is for you to judge, as you read on, whether that desire was realised.

2
NOT IN THE HOLIDAY BROCHURES

You could say that it was not a very appropriate time to take a holiday, as Eileen was still feeling desperately tired. However, at that time we did not know that anything was seriously wrong, and hoped that, if Eileen spent the holiday quietly, she would emerge from it feeling refreshed.

A year earlier, Eileen's sister Betty and her husband, Winston, had booked a holiday on the Algarve; but, because of Betty's serious illness, they had invited us to take their place. Now, a year later, they wanted to see the area for themselves: they had booked an apartment, and invited us to take the adjoining one. That was why we found ourselves in early October driving with them to Dublin in order to board a flight to Faro.

Arriving in bright sunshine, we picked up the hire car and drove to Portimao, where we were to stay. Like many holiday destinations, it was a delightful piece of previously unspoiled coastline, which had spawned a plethora of hotels and apartments. Ours was a nondescript building that afforded access to the sea if you walked some 200 yards up a gently sloping road, and then descended steps to the beach.

That first night we were disturbed by noisy fellow guests and by construction workers who made use of the first crack of light. That is what holidays are all about – exchanging our home comforts for deprivations and inconveniences in order to enjoy the bonus of some warm sunshine.

That first morning we drove to Lagos – not the Nigerian version, but a local one pronounced 'Lag-os'. A year earlier we had visited the place in pouring rain. Now, in brilliant sunshine, we were able to take advantage of the glorious little cove of the Praia d'Ann. We had a refreshing bathe in the turquoise ocean, followed by a meal in a restaurant that overlooked the beach.

From here we drove to Sagres. The fortress of Henry the Navigator looked so unprepossessing on the outside that we did not feel disposed to pay money in order to see more of the same on the inside. It was then just a short drive to the Cape of Vicente, with its prominent lighthouse, which marked the south west tip of Europe.

In my prayer time the next morning I was reading about how God helped Paul when he was facing storms at sea; and reflected that he was still able to help us when facing our own storms.

That morning we inspected a marina that was not far away. The boats, with their reflections in the calm water, were very photogenic. Winston and I climbed the stairs of a former castle to get a better view, while the ladies remained at ground level.

We took the car to the centre of Portimao. Once again it was left to the men to explore the main features, which included an elaborate fountain. A bank was called Banco da Espiritu Sancto. It sounded like a safe place to leave your money in a time of economic turmoil.

Because of deterioration in the weather, we ventured no further that afternoon than the health centre in our apartment block. We had to buy and wear a plastic skull-cap, which I found irksome, especially as I had no hair to cover. As well as the pool, we visited the sauna and the steam room, but I had to give Eileen a lot of help because of her condition. We took the car to a local restaurant that evening because of the rain.

On Wednesday we drove to Monchique, up in the hills, and well away from the tourist-dominated coastal area. While Eileen rested in the car, the three of us took a walk round the town. We inspected the interior of a large church, but were not impressed when we found it was dominated by a statue of Mary.

We followed a mountain road to Aljezur. About half way, we came upon a wayside restaurant and decided to go inside. The waiter, who had a good command of English, gave us free samples of the two main dishes. We liked these so much that we ordered both. We had planned to drive on to the beaches of the west coast, but the uneven roads had so jolted Betty that it was thought better to return to base and give the ladies a rest.

On Thursday we took a cruise up the river from Portimao to Silves. Our journey in a cool breeze took us past a nature reserve, where storks perched on posts or wheeled about overhead. There were grey herons and cormorants, and some people even thought they spotted eagles. Once again, on arrival, Winston and I explored widely, while the ladies remained in the riverside area.

That afternoon, Eileen simply wanted to rest. We were to have visited the health spa again, but she had been vomiting and felt miserable. Instead of going out with the others for an evening meal, I stayed with Eileen. We sent a text message to our close friend Jo-Joy asking for her prayers. For a time I held her in my arms as a physical form of prayer. Within half an hour the pain had gone, and the nausea had disappeared; but it was as if we had passed a watershed, and things would never be quite the same again.

*

A few months earlier, when Eileen and I were walking along the coast near our home, we found ourselves talking about the future. When the time came, we observed, one of us would have to die first, and it would be hard for the one that was left. "I will probably go first", I suggested. "Men do not normally live as long as women."

We were not being morbid, but realistic. One of us would have to face this separation one day. It happens in all marriages. As we both led very healthy lifestyles, however, we did not anticipate that this would happen for a long time. We might even be able to celebrate our Golden Wedding in 2022! Or so it seemed.

When that time of separation came, there were various ways in which it might happen. It might be that one of us would die suddenly: that would be fine for the one who died, but a dreadful shock for the partner who was left. It might be after a long illness, which would be hard to endure, but would give ample opportunity to say goodbye. Or it might be that one of us would get Alzheimers, and there would be no clear-cut moment of goodbye. If anything, the third option was the one most to be feared: we had seen this happen to some of our friends.

During this holiday, we were reading and enjoying a thriller called 'No Time for Goodbye'. This was not an option that we would enjoy. We wanted to be able to say our goodbyes properly. That, in effect, is how things would turn out.

But here, as we lay together, these future developments were hidden from us. All I knew was that Eileen was sick, and needed the comfort of my presence.

*

I did not attempt the next day to go with Winston and Betty on their outing. Instead, I visited the local beach for a little while and spent the rest of the time with Eileen. She felt well enough in the late afternoon to spend some time at the health suite.

The following day was much the same. I remained behind so as to be with Eileen. A coastal walk and a swim in the local pool were adventure enough in the circumstances. Later, when Winston, Betty and I returned from our meal, we brought soup for Eileen, which she took a little at a time. At various times that day we prayed that Eileen would be well enough for the return journey on the morrow.

At the airport we had to queue for an hour and a quarter just to check in. Immediately in front of us was a party of golfers from County Mayo. Fortunately, the ladies were able to remain seated until we were free to move on. During the flight, Eileen required water to take her paracetamol, but to our dismay the stewardess said it would only be available when the snacks trolley came round. We were thankful to arrive in Dublin, where we picked up the car and drove back to Ballynahinch. It was my turn, then, to make the last 50 minute drive to our own home.

We were so thankful that God had answered our prayer and got us home safely. We were glad also that Eileen's hospital appointment was almost upon us, as it ought to answer a lot of questions.

3
TALES OF THE UNEXPECTED

There was just one thing to be done on the day before the hospital appointment: we went to see our GP to receive a prescription for tablets that would reduce the nausea.

The next day, after an early lunch, I took Eileen to the day procedure unit at the Ards Community Hospital, some 9 miles away from our home. As it was likely to be a lengthy procedure, I was encouraged to go home and collect her some time later. This I did. When I returned, I was informed that she was not yet ready: they had decided not only to inspect the bowels but also to inspect the stomach by putting a scope down through the throat.

We were asked to stay behind for a while, as the consultant wanted to speak to us. This sounded a bit ominous, but neither of us was ready for the full import of what was to take place. After a period of waiting, we were ushered into a small room, where both the consultant, Dr. Marshall, and a nurse joined us.

From the sound of his voice, we knew that he was very concerned for us. "I'm afraid I have to tell you," he said, "that we have discovered several ulcers in your stomach, and they are likely to be malignant." It was not a definite pronouncement of doom, but he would not have mentioned that possibility had it been only a remote one. From the first moment, however, Eileen had an incredible peace. This would remain with her virtually all the time as the illness progressed. On this first day she called to mind the words of Isaiah 54:17: "No weapon forged against you will prevail".

I had often been moved by a poem of John Betjeman's called 'Devonshire Street W1' in which a couple receive similar news:
> "No hope. And the X-ray photographs under his arm
> Confirm the message. His wife stands timidly by."
In the poem they try to ignore the severity of the situation by talking calmly about which bus they should catch. .

I suppose many of us wonder how we would react to such news if it happened to us. There is no way of knowing until it becomes your own story. Unlike the couple in the poem, we had a clear faith. That is how Eileen was able to enjoy such peace. For myself, I was to react with a whole gamut of emotions. Even when we are Christians, we are still human beings, and I was very conscious of my limitations. God is no hard taskmaster, expecting us to be shining examples of pure trust under such extreme conditions. He understood my weakness as I tried to absorb this news, and I believe he undergirded me with his love, because he cared for me.

The next hurdle would be a CT scan, which it was hoped would make the situation a lot clearer; but it looked as if we would have to wait two weeks for this. How could we endure such a long period of waiting? This was to prove one of the biggest difficulties that faced us – the necessity to wait time and time again for a next stage, without any knowledge of the outcome. Waiting for clarification, waiting for the next decision, waiting for the next course of treatment, waiting for some evidence of improvement.... waiting, waiting, waiting.

I had a fertile imagination. Already I was thinking how hard it would be to face life without Eileen. Yet here she was living and breathing beside me. How could I dare to think like this? That was a defeatist attitude. I arranged for someone else to lead the discussion group at Greyabbey so that I could spend the evening with Eileen.

I slept well until 3, but could hardly sleep after that. That was how I dealt with things. If I had anything on my mind, it would not usually stop me from getting to sleep; but in the early hours I would wake up with this matter in the forefront of my thinking, and further sleep was impossible.

During my morning jog, I was bawling like a child. Virtually every day since, I have given way to tears. I had long been a phlegmatic character. If Eileen and I were watching a two-handkerchief television programme, Eileen's eyes would fill with tears, but I would remain unmoved. She would steal a glance of mock disapproval at me. It had long been a joke between us. Only occasionally, as , for instance, at the end of 'The Killing Fields' would the tears well up in my eyes. But from this time onwards, tears would be a normal part of my life.

I make no apology for this. I see tears as the flipside of love. If you truly love somebody, you do not like to see them hurt; and the very whisper of possible separation plays havoc with the emotions. I would weep to see Eileen suffering; I would weep for my own mental suffering; I would weep for both of us, in view of the possible ending of an earthly relationship that had been so precious and fulfilling.

Those tears also served a very positive purpose. They enabled me to give in to my emotions in private so that I could be strong in public. The apparent bravery, the ability to cope, the making of good decisions, the daily patience, the acceptance of a wholly new way of life – these and other positive features would not have been possible without the gift of tears.

I see in my life also another use for tears. At the age of 18 I went to Cambridge to take the entrance examination. That first night away from home I unexpectedly found myself crying bitterly. I suppose it was the realization that my life was about to change, and that I would no longer live comfortably in my parental home that triggered things off. Most of us fear change and wonder whether we shall be able to cope. After that, I was able to cope with my new life in other places. The tears of that evening set me up to accept and embrace change. Bereavement, however, is the biggest change that any of us will have to face.

I came back from that first tearful jog to read some verses from Psalm 13: "Answer me, O Lord my God; give me light in my darkness lest I die." "But I will always trust in you and your mercy and shall rejoice in your salvation."

I began to read to Eileen regularly from the journal which I have kept for more than half a century. We began with the story of how we first came together.

*

When I went as a missionary to Taiwan in 1969, the plan was that, after two years of language study, I would move to my real work in Sabah. These plans were frustrated when I was denied a visa to enter the country. Having enjoyed some student ministry during my time in Taipei, I was happy to move to Tainan, in the south of the country, to run a student hostel called St. Michael's House and to teach in the university. On my first Sunday there, a little group of Americans came to the hostel to sing and give their testimonies. Both Chinese and Westerners attended this event. One of the guests who signed my visitors' book on that day was a Belfast girl called Eileen Gordon.

*

On Wednesdays, Eileen normally attended her patchwork class in Bangor. As she was in no position to drive herself, on this occasion I took her there. I was glad I had done so, for her friends there gave her a lot of tender loving care.

They asked if she wanted to put her name down for their Christmas dinner, but she declined. Afterwards she explained to me that she did not even know whether she would be alive at that time. I could not get my head round this.

Our son, Chris, had been doing his own research on the internet, based on the information we had given him. "In 8 cases out of 10", he said confidently on the 'phone, "ulcers can be cleared up in a few weeks." We had not told our sons how serious the situation was, lest the diagnosis should not be confirmed, and we would prove to have worried them without reason. As our relationships had always been marked by complete honesty, it was very hard for us to keep this back from them. This made such conversations all the more poignant.

Lying awake in bed at 2.30am, I sensed that Eileen was experiencing discomfort, and thought of those words in Isaiah 43: "Fear not, for I have redeemed you; I have called you by name; you are mine. When you pass through the waters, I will be with you...."

Winston and Betty came on a surprise visit; and Andrew and Jmin called us on Skype from Seoul. On both occasions we sought to sound more cheerful than we really felt.

As Eileen did not feel well enough to attend the weekly prayer meeting at church, we stayed at home and watched documentaries on television. I kept stealing a glance in Eileen's direction. I found it hard to believe that she might no longer be a presence beside me. It was like a nightmare.

*

As a little group of five missionaries, we met on Sunday evenings for Bible Study and prayer. As Eileen was a member of this group, we got to know each other better. What I did not know at the time was that people had been dropping hints to Eileen about getting to know this eligible bachelor who had come into the midst, and that she was determined to resist this. At that time there was no suggestion that ours would develop into a close relationship. It was not the old story of love at first sight.

*

Eileen felt she might be able to eat some Rice Krispies and keep them down; so I went to a local shop to buy some. On the way back, I met a casual acquaintance in the street. He cheerily cried: "How are you? Eileen feeling better?" But he was out of earshot before I had a chance to reply.

We had some good news that afternoon. I was doing some pastoral visiting in Kircubbin, when Eileen called to say she had just heard from Mr. Marshall: the scan would now take place on Monday, considerably earlier than originally planned. When I got home there was more news: the Bishop called to say that a new incumbent would look after Greyabbey and Kircubbin from 4 December onwards, and my tenure of nearly three years would thus soon be over. This was good for me, as Eileen's needs would now take priority over pastoral work.

By this time, both Eileen and I had experienced a raising of the spirits. The heavy burden of grief had been removed and we had entered upon a period of rest. Eileen even felt well enough to help me prepare the supper. While jogging the next morning I was able to recall God's promise, "My grace is sufficient for you".

When Kevin, our Rector, called that afternoon, it was typical of Eileen that she wanted to talk about God's work in the peninsula more than her illness. She was delighted to hear that various clergy were coming together for discussion and prayer.

*

I joined an American group called Toastmasters, which was for people who enjoyed public speaking. At their dinner in January I needed to take someone with me. Eileen agreed to be that person. It was the first time we had been seen in public together. Some even innocently called her 'Mrs Taylor'.

Actually, that did not seem a bad idea. We met together more often, and a bond of friendship grew up between us. We had meals together, played Scrabble, and even began tentatively to discuss the possibility that it would lead to marriage.

*

At the Sunday services, I announced the appointment of the new Rector. The people were delighted to hear the good news. Although it was perfect timing for me, I nevertheless already began to feel a sense of bereavement, as I had grown close to these people in the almost three years that I had served them.

Meanwhile Eileen, with the help of a neighbour, had managed to get to our local church. Finding that the congregation was struggling with the hymn, 'In Christ alone', she went to the front to give them a lead. What a wonderful wife I had!

Unlike Eileen, however, I found it hard to maintain a feeling of peace. That Sunday afternoon, despite the strong wind, I felt the need to go for a short walk along the shoreline, and to cry out to God to give me such peace.

*

One day in March 1972 I wrote in the journal:

> *"Eileen came with the dogs and we went out for a walk. The first part was on Da Tung Road, so it was very noisy. When we turned off to walk along roads and tracks by sugar cane fields, it was much more pleasant. Eileen and I talked about our position. After our return she made me some coffee. The experience left me heavy hearted. Was it a fear that I was doing the wrong thing? Was it a fear that I might not be able to do all that was required of a lover and a husband? My conclusion was that I must pray much more, so that I do not stray from God's purpose. This experience involves another person beside myself, and the last thing I want to do is hurt her."*

*

On Monday I took Eileen to the Ulster Hospital for her CT scan. She had to drink a large beaker of pink liquid, which was a trial in itself, before the scan could take place. We were anxious to know the results as soon as possible. But, of course, there was to be more waiting....

Gregor had recently become chaplain to retired clergy and their wives. Although he lived nearly an hour away by car, he came to see us that afternoon, and he made several subsequent visits. We respected the warm pastoral heart that led him to do this.

When we called Andrew in Seoul that same day to wish him a happy birthday, he said to his mother: : "My greatest present would be to know that you are well." How we longed to share the whole situation with him!

25

*

One day in May I wrote:

"We had supper at Eileen's. It was not her most successful creation! Afterwards we discussed an article about deciding when you have fallen in love from the magazine 'His'. I think Eileen regards me as too self-analytical, for I am always saying I don't have the love I ought to have."

*

We both had a bad night. Around 4am Eileen asked me to ring the out-of-hours doctor. He advised me to try the pills again, and if this failed he would come and give her an injection. We prayed as she took the medicine, and it worked. Later on, JoJoy told us that she had woken at 4 with an urge to pray for Eileen.

It meant a lot to Eileen that I was able to get her to her hairdresser's in Ballynahinch, even though it meant a drive of 50 minutes each way. She needed to have a normal activity in the midst of so much abnormality. Afterwards she made an appointment for a date six weeks later. I wondered if she would still be around to keep it. We had lunch at Winston and Betty's house. They showed us pictures of the Algarve holiday on the screen, but they did not hold very pleasant memories for me.

Later in the day I picked up a friend called Rosemary from the airport. Like Eileen, she had served for a long time with the Overseas Missionary Fellowship. Now she was ordained and living in Cardiff. It was useful to leave her with Eileen while I attended the discipleship class in Greyabbey.

*

One hot, sunny day, Eileen and I cycled to the beach together. After our bathe, we discussed a book I was reading about sexual happiness in marriage. It was a new, untrodden yet exciting prospect.

*

The next morning, Rosemary went with me to buy two nightdresses for Eileen, just in case she should have to go into hospital. It turned out to be a wise provision.

26

We planned to go to a healing meeting in Carryduff. Eileen was very anxious to go, but I was concerned that it would place a lot of physical strain on her. As it happened, we never got there. Instead, as I was preparing supper, there was a telephone call from the consultant, Dr. Marshall, informing us that he would like to talk with us face to face. That again sounded ominous. We met him, as arranged, on Ward 7 of the Ulster Hospital. He told us that, according to the scan, Eileen had cancer in the stomach, kidneys, spleen and the bones, and that it appeared to be a lymphoma, which was treatable by chemotherapy. What puzzled him, however, was that there was also cancer in the ovaries, an area not usually infected by a lymphoma. Further investigation was required. "Would you like to come into hospital for a few days while we take a look at this?" he invited. It seemed a good idea.

Accordingly, we returned home to collect the things she needed. When she had settled into her hospital bed a telephone was brought to her. It was our son, Chris, full of anxious questions. As Eileen spoke words of reassurance to him, there was such a serenity about her.

4
A SHOCK TO THE SYSTEM

The night after Eileen's admission to hospital, I slept only patchily. When I opened the Bible I was comforted by the words from 2 Chronicles 15: "The Lord will stay with you as long as you stay with him! Whenever you look for him, you will find him."

I would take such encouragements from the scriptures with me to the hospital and share them with Eileen. As it was now hard for Eileen to search the scriptures for herself, I had to do this for both of us. Often it was to be passages from the Psalms which leaped out from the page and met us at the point of need.

That morning there was to be a visit to a new development called Maxwell's Courtyard in Kircubbin of Mary McAleese, the President of Ireland, and I had been invited to attend. My body was there, but my mind was in the hospital with Eileen. Our distinguished visitor had dignity and poise, and she had the ability to make meaningful conversation with all kinds of people. I was glad I had met her. Afterwards she gave a short speech about the importance of volunteers to our communities.

When I rejoined Eileen, I found that her new medication had removed the pain and nausea, and she was feeling better than she had done for days. Winston and Betty came on a visit, and the two sisters were able to chat and laugh together as if nothing was wrong.

I took Rosemary back to the hospital with me in the evening. The Bishop came on the first of many visits. With the additional visit of Kevin, our Rector, Eileen had had five clergy to pray with her on one day!

*

Eileen and I were spending more and more time together. One day we went to Kaohsiung to do some shopping, and I began to learn that patience which would serve me well in later years. Another time we went to Pingtung, so that I could prepare an article on St. Mark's Church. On another occasion we visited the bamboo factory in Kuan Miao.

A longer excursion was an overnight stay at the home of some friends who lived on the Tunghai campus in Taichung, in the centre of the island. Joan took a bus to town with us to help us choose an engagement ring. It was not that we were officially engaged, but we wanted to be ready for that possibility. At one shop we bought an aquamarine stone, at another some diamond chips; then we went to the shop of a man affectionately known as 'Gooey', and he promised to do the setting within 24 hours. He was as good as his word, and the next day we collected a most attractive ring of Victorian Gold, which would later attract much admiration.

*

There was a switch the next day: Rosemary had to leave for a conference, but I collected JoJoy from the airport and brought her to see Eileen. Various 'professionals' had come to her bedside to offer their expertise. What irked us was the two hour gap between afternoon and evening visiting, when all we could do was sit around the hospital waiting.

It was at this time that I began to feel the symptoms of 'shock'. This was not in the medical sense, but more in a psychological sense. Emotionally, I was finding it hard to react appropriately to what was taking place around me. For instance, on the way home JoJoy wanted to call at a supermarket in a large shopping centre in order to buy things which she thought might be helpful to Eileen. I found this very stressful. All around me were people enjoying normal life. I wanted to shout: "Why are you all so occupied with trivialities? Don't you realize that we are dealing with matters of life and death?"

I recall a time when, as a student, I was working in a grocery store. One day I took a delivery of groceries to an elderly lady. I found her sitting by the fireside, stunned at the news she had just received of her son's death. Suddenly from outside came the cheery jingle of an ice cream van.

Auden, in his poem, 'Musee des Beaux Arts', describes a painting of Icarus, his wings melted by the sun, falling to his death. He writes:
> "In Brueghel's *Icarus*, for instance: how everything turns away
> Quite leisurely from the disaster; the ploughman may
> Have heard the splash, the forsaken cry.
> But for him it was not an important failure...."

I see the same effect in Edwin Muir's poem, 'The Interrogation', in which the writer and his companions are being questioned at a border checkpoint while normal life goes on elsewhere:

"The careless lovers in pairs go by,
Hand linked in hand, wandering another star,
So near we could shout to them."

So I was going through my trauma in the world which was occupied with its own business, and, for a while, that was hard to take.

The same feeling grabbed me the next day. On the way to hospital for our afternoon visit, JoJoy wanted to buy a jumper in the crowded shopping centre. Visiting time had begun and I was still waiting for her to return. Once again I felt very tense.

I had problems again in the evening. Chris and Lauri arrived by plane. After the evening visiting we needed food, I was prepared to get something simple together at home, but the others wanted to go to an inn near the hospital. It was the sort of place people would go for a pleasant evening out. All around me were people enjoying their leisure time, and all I wanted to do was to find somewhere quiet and peaceful. Yes, for me this really was a time of stress.

*

For our last outing in Taiwan as a courting couple, we went back to the lake which was the scene of our first outing. There we hired a boat. The journey out was fine, but a contrary wind made the return journey rather slow.

Within a few days we would be starting out for the UK. The Lord had so arranged it that our furloughs coincided. The tickets to Hong Kong were in our possession, but the reduced rate tickets from Hong Kong to London had not yet arrived. There was still a little time left; but when the day of our journey came round we had not received them. We would have to go out in faith, hoping to put things right in Hong Kong. This was another kind of stress.

On arrival in Hong Kong we went to stay with Eileen's friend Evelyn in a flat which had the security of Fort Knox. During this visit I was able to observe Eileen not just in the later part of the day but also in

30

the early morning when she was not at her best; but somehow our relationship survived the test.

One of the pleasant parts of our stay was a visit we made to Cheung-Chao Island. It was a most romantic place to do our courting. How fortunate we were!

*

All four of us went to Greyabbey for the morning service. As I was feeling fragile, I had asked a friend to conduct the service so that I would only have to preach. The Lord enabled me to speak of our current situation without shedding a tear. Chris went with me to Kircubbin, where I repeated the sermon. When we got back to the house, we found that the ladies had prepared a special meal through which we could celebrate Eileen's life together. A pity she was not there to share it with us! When we saw her, however, we were pleased to see that she was in better shape, having eaten more than previously.

On Monday morning I had to take JoJoy back to the airport. She was late getting away and we were racing against time. More tension! However, when I got back home I found that Chris and Lauri were giving the house a good clean for me. It was good to see that quality of love and care expressed in a practical way.

Eileen was in a good mood that afternoon. I read to her about our time on Cheung-Chao Island and the other ladies on our section of the ward listened intently as well. They talked with us too of the Christian faith and we ended up praying for the whole group. It was good to see that Eileen and I had opportunity for witness in this way. I don't think we would have been easily forgotten.

That evening, just after the Bishop's visit, we learned that a bed had been made available for Eileen at the City Hospital. It was good that Chris and Lauri were there to help get her ready. The woman in the bed opposite told us, before we left, how God had healed her of cancer. The inference was that he could do the same for us. As no ambulance was available, we had to use the car to get Eileen from one hospital to the other – a journey of about 20 minutes to the other side of Belfast.

5
PUZZLE CORNER

When we went the next day to see Eileen in her new ward in the Tower Block at City Hospital, we found her well settled and in good spirits. These sad events were bringing us all closer together. We spent part of the time reading about our further adventures in Hong Kong.

Just as we were about to leave, we heard that a surgeon wanted to speak with us. We gathered in a small room just inside the ward entrance, and he told us of his plan to remove the ovaries on the afternoon of the next day, provided that Eileen's blood count was high enough. This was major surgery. It would also give opportunity to look at other places affected by cancer and to decide what to do about it.

I felt angry that this cancer should attack such a wonderful wife. In fact, anger was for me a strong emotion. I do not think I was angry with God. Even if I had been, I am sure he could have taken it: he would prefer that we express our anger and frustration in his presence rather than ignoring him. My anger was rather against the disease itself. Although I am not given to profanity, I found myself in private swearing at the cancer. This had no practical value, but it enabled me to express my feelings. How did this cancer dare to invade the body of someone who had served God so well and who still had so much to give? I am in good company, for such things made Jesus angry as well.

During the evening visiting, the shadow of the forthcoming operation lay upon us. In fact, the operation did not take place. It was one of a number of suggested tactics that were never carried out. It was as if the medical staff were trying to find the solution to a major puzzle and not having much success with it.

*

Our main concern during our time in Hong Kong was to get hold of the tickets. At the Far East Travel Agency we were told that our names were not on the list of passengers. In the end we enlisted the aid of Eileen's missionary society (OMF). They managed to make a new booking for us. We hoped to be able to reimburse them when we got a refund from the original booking. Strangely enough, it looked as if we were on the very flight we had booked for in the first place.

I could happily describe the Star Ferry, Stanley Beach, the Repulse Bay Hotel, the refugee community of Rennie's Mill and other places that we visited, but this would take too long. It is sufficient to record that, after a delightful week together, we boarded our 'plane for the long journey back to the UK.

*

The next morning I took Chris and Lauri back to the airport to catch their flight home. On the way back I did some shopping at Sainsbury's. It was a poignant affair, for I would have always done this shopping with Eileen. After this, I did my weekly shopping mostly at a branch of Tesco's, firstly because it was nearer, and secondly because it held for me no wistful memories of Eileen.

Left to myself, I began a new regime of driving to Bangor and taking the train from there, as there was a station in the hospital itself. It was on my arrival that afternoon that I discovered Eileen had not had the operation. There was need first of all to ensure that the kidneys were working better, and they had fitted a stent. They might attempt the bigger operation in a few days' time. Nothing was certain. I prayed to God for a miracle; then we read the account of our journey from Hong Kong back to England.

*

Eileen and I had a couple of hours together in the centre of London before she was due to catch her flight to Belfast. We treated ourselves to some strawberries and cream at a little place by the Marble Arch. As the cream in Taiwan was often synthetic, Eileen asked, "Is this real cream?" The waiter was surprised that anyone should feel the need to ask such a question.

*

I had planned to attend part of a missionary prayer meeting the following morning; but when I received a message that Eileen was weepy, I went straight to the hospital. Although it was not the official visiting time, I was given a special dispensation. She was already much better, having derived comfort from a visit by Kevin.

33

Before afternoon visiting, I went into town to buy new headphones for Eileen, as she liked to listen to Christian music. Normally, she would gain much from her reading of the Bible and good Christian books, but, under the duress of her illness, she lacked the necessary concentration. Music lifted her spirits and drew her nearer to God. I also bought a new recording by Stuart Townend, a favourite composer and performer of ours. We shared some Bible verses, and read about the time when I proposed to her.

*

Separated by the Irish Sea, we communicated by letter. Eileen told me how her mother had warded off a gang of rioters who wanted to burn down the business next door.

Before making the engagement official, we both went to take a look at our prospective mothers-in-law. First Eileen came to Blackpool to meet my mother, and after three days it was my turn to go to Belfast to meet hers. We both liked what we saw.

On the Saturday we visited Tollymore Park, at the foot of the Mournes. Beside Foley's Bridge there was a little shelter, and it was there that I officially proposed. There was no question of my being refused. I slipped the ring on her finger: we were now engaged. When we got back to Eileen's parents' home, an engagement present was already waiting for us. They had had no doubt about the outcome.

*

That evening, as we talked, Eileen said that, when she was led to consider what she was seeking in her prayers, the answer was 'More of God'. "Cancer has touched my body," she said, "but it cannot touch my spirit." This was her testimony throughout her illness. We also learned today that the plans for major surgery had been abandoned, as Eileen's body was now in too weak a state to face it.

The next day, Eileen had many visits from friends and 'professionals', all offering help; but this left her very tired. I had some respite in Lisburn, where a family friend picked me up from the station and gave me a meal. When I returned, Eileen and I found ourselves talking about the funeral. I longed from the depths of my heart that there would not be such an occasion for a long time, but we had to be realistic. The signs were bleak. What I found hard was my inability to protect Eileen from harm at a time when she was so helpless.

It was around this time that I wrote a eulogy about Eileen and stored it on the computer. I hoped desperately that I would not need to use it; but I was aware that, if and when Eileen was taken from me, I might be in no position to compose a eulogy at that time.

When I was a curate in Blackburn in the 1960s, I visited the home of a man who had lost one wife with cancer, and who was about to lose a second wife to the same disease. He was naturally very bitter about it. He was also determined not to let his wife know that her condition was terminal. This made it very difficult to minister effectively in that situation. It was like walking on eggshells.

Eileen and I resolved, all through this experience, that we would be absolutely straight with other people. We hoped through our witness to show that cancer was not something to talk about in hushed whispers, but to be faced fairly and squarely. This, for me, was not incompatible with tears; but, in a strange sort of way, those tears gave me strength for my open witness.

On the first day of the new month, Eileen had a lot of visitors, and this proved tiring. She really appreciated seeing people, but was thankful when the visits were short. We tried to make our friends aware of this. That evening there were just the two of us. We read from the journal about various visits we had made in London in September 1972. Part of the time we simply held hands.

*

At the CMS headquarters on Waterloo Road, there was a special day for missionaries on furlough. Some 25 of us met together to get a re-introduction into life in the UK. We learned about changes in the Anglican Church and the position of the Ugandan Asians.

The next day we went to the headquarters of the Church Pastoral Aid Society to discuss with a friend who worked there the contents of a book we were writing about missionary support. At that time, great interest was shown in the project; but later that interest was withdrawn, and the book was never published.

That same afternoon we returned to CMS so that Eileen could be interviewed. Although she had served faithfully with OMF for many years, that did not necessarily make her an acceptable candidate for CMS. We hoped for a happy outcome, and had not really considered what we would do in the unlikely event that CMS did not approve of her.

The following day we visited the OMF headquarters, then in Newington Green, but shortly afterwards to move to Sevenoaks. Eileen was able to tell them something about the current situation in Taiwan. Later on, we visited a 'left-handed shop': you almost felt as if you had to look cautiously to right and left before going in.

For recreation we went to the Tower of London, where Eileen was greatly impressed by the Crown Jewels; but she allowed them to remain intact.

*

I slept better, and, as I ran, I felt spiritually and mentally stronger. Later, while sitting in my chair, I saw an endless stream of birds (probably starlings) flying from left to right across the sky, and even began to recover some of my joy in the Lord. This was a good preparation for the day's worship services.

When I saw Eileen that afternoon she had good news to share: the potassium level was down, thus enabling her to eat better; and the kidneys were now working properly. There was a possibility that the mass on the ovaries was just a cluster of benign cysts, but the truth would be revealed through Wednesday's biopsy.

It was hard to get the balance when administering pain-killing drugs. If she had too much, it made her sleepy; if too little, then it might not be properly effective.

Around this time I also bought Eileen a book of Matt cartoons. This 'Telegraph' cartoonist never failed to amuse us, and Eileen got many laughs out of reading this book. I was so happy that I could bring her pleasure and even hear her laugh. Life together had always been fun, and we had no desire to give up on that now.

*

There followed another period of separation. One day I took my mother to Preston so that she could choose an outfit for the wedding. I did deputation ministry in Cumbria on my own.

We were together again when Eileen went before the CMS Candidates' Committee in London. To our relief it was announced that they would be happy to welcome her into the CMS family. If they had been unwilling to accept her, we would have been in a quandary. We parted again – Eileen to do a little secretarial work for the mission in London and myself to do some deputation in Cambridge. I was a guest at top table in my old college. I had often wondered what distinguished topics the dons discussed together: on this day it was the long hair of male students.

Eileen joined me again for a link visit to St. Edmund's, Whalley Range, in Manchester. The people of that church had given me plenty of support, and were now delighted to meet Eileen as well. When we separated this time, we knew we would not see each other again until the time of the wedding.

*

My 71st birthday was not a very typical one. In the morning I celebrated Communion in the historic chapel at Mount Stewart, a National Trust property. Both sons called me during the day to give me personal greetings.

On our birthdays we would normally go out for a special meal together. This time it was not possible. As Eileen's biopsy had been conducted under local anaesthetic, she was free to receive visitors this afternoon. I was getting worried about her weight loss: she looked so frail when I helped her to walk to the bathroom. We read together about our wedding and honeymoon, and it brought the memories flooding back.

*

The service took place on a cold November day in Belmont Presbyterian, as Eileen's old church was at that time occupied by soldiers. I have never been inside that building either before or since. We had two Presbyterian ministers and one Anglican friend to ensure that everything was done properly. When I called out 'I will' loudly and clearly, everybody was made vividly aware of my intentions. So we pledged to love one another, with all that this would involve, until death should separate us.

The reception took place at an establishment called Abbeyfield in Whiteabbey, which later became a home for the elderly. Because of the bad weather, most of the photographs were taken indoors. The meal was followed by good quality speeches. In those days people did not have evening parties, so we were free to drive the car which Eileen's father had lent us to Portballintrae on the north coast for our honeymoon. £44 for a week's full board seemed a lot at the time. Nowadays it would not even cover us for a day.

When I look back to that honeymoon, I reflect how little we really knew one another. It took us a while to learn the techniques for expressing our love physically, but it was fun trying. Because of the weather, we did not have many outings: it was a matter of eating big meals and getting better acquainted. Recently we found ourselves in Portballintrae again during a walking holiday; but we discovered that the hotel had been pulled down.

*

When I saw Eileen on the Thursday she did not feel at all well, and considered this to be a spiritual attack; for Kevin had brought the encouraging news that morning that peninsula clergy were to meet together to prepare the first combined praise gathering. She looked a little better the next day,

On Saturday, observing how hard it was for Eileen to keep her food down, I wrote in the journal:
> *"I am worried that she is not getting the nourishment she needs. I hate to see her reduced to this little world of a bed and a few paltry belonging, I would love to take her off on a white charger to a bold and spacious place. She does not deserve this, and my heart is in agony."*

Apart from her not being fit to make such a journey, I did not know how to ride a white charger.

On Sunday morning, as I read of Nehemiah's concern for Jerusalem, I thought of Eileen's deep burden for the Ards peninsula. I preached that morning at the

38

Belfast Chinese Church. Wai Kuen, who was leading, prayed publicly for Eileen.

We knew that we needed all the prayer we could get. I would send out regular information about Eileen to a group of praying friends. Some of them even suggested to me that I was doing them a favour by writing to them so regularly with news of Eileen. I am sure that one reason we were given strength to face our situation was the volume of prayer in many countries that was going up for us.

That evening Eileen and I had a good time together. The lady in the next bed said she been much helped by a verse from a psalm which I had read to Eileen. We were both in a positive mood. Hopefully, a prognosis would be given in the next few days.

One thing that was hard for Eileen at that time was to watch people come and go. The doctors were still perplexed about the way ahead, and she herself had become very frail. She was dependent on a driver for the relief of pain, and this had to be inspected at regular intervals. In such a condition, would she ever, I wondered, be fit to return home. So the long wait continued, and we did not know how it would end.

The weather was cold and windy. It was as if it was in sympathy with our own wintry circumstances. A woman came to talk with Eileen about palliative care. At least, it looked as if someone contemplated a life beyond this hospital ward.

One day I wrote in the journal:
"I am not very good at making close friendships. The exception is my relationship with Eileen, which has been brilliant. But if that relationship is to end, that leaves me in a very lonely position. That is one reason why I feel such grief. But it grieves me also to see Eileen as only a shadow of her normal vibrant self."

*

It was still the early days of working on that relationship. After our honeymoon we spent a few days with Eileen's folks in Ireland; then we took the ferry across to Heysham and drove over the Pennines to get to a lunch meeting in Durham. Two days later we were in Blackburn. So it went on. We were adapting not only to our life together, but also to a variety of settings.

A few days later, we went to Foxbury, a CMS conference centre in Chislehurst. We used this as a base from which we could visit various friends and relatives in Islington, Harrow, Blackheath, Maidstone and elsewhere. Staying at such a place could have its disadvantages: one day we were enjoying a time of intimacy when some men came to inspect the plumbing! Finally, at CMS headquarters, we were commissioned for the work which lay ahead.

*

Eileen called me on Wednesday morning to tell me that the consultant had informed her that the tissue taken from the ovaries was not enough to yield a result, and there would therefore be need for another biopsy. My initial reaction to this news was anger. It meant that our time of waiting was prolonged further.

That repeat procedure took place the next day, five minutes after my arrival. While she was away, I went to the chapel for a time of prayer. The Lord gave me the closing verses of Isaiah 40 and 1 Peter 5:7 to encourage me. When I returned to the ward, Eileen was not yet back; but the consultant told me that it was a good biopsy, and he thought it likely that the mass on the ovaries was not cancerous. This news lifted my spirits. Life had become like a rollercoaster.

There were three more days of undramatic visits. I did not stay with Eileen as long as usual because I had a heavy cold.

*

The first crisis in our married life came at the Stranraer ferry terminal, when we were going to Ulster for Christmas. I insisted that we did not need to book in to join the ferry queue; but when we came near the boat we were turned back because of this, and had to wait for the next ferry. This was not good for our relationship!

We were driving a friend's car, and had done so up to that point without incident. As we were boarding the ferry, however, we were directed to a spot where there was a protruding nail, which scratched the bodywork. I looked to the purser to arrange compensation, but did not look forward to explaining to our friend what had happened.

40

During that Christmas, spent with Eileen's folks, when we were not eating and drinking, we were making a rug for our future home.

*

On Tuesday there was talk of going home! Eileen and I went to the Occupational Therapy Department, where we were shown various devices which would make life more comfortable for her upon her return. The downside was that it meant Eileen would be living as an invalid. I hoped this would just be a temporary phase. That evening we read about our first Christmas together as man and wife.

To celebrate our wedding anniversary on the 18th, we ate ice lollies. This was a far cry from the usual meal in a good restaurant, but it was better than nothing. I took our wedding album into the hospital so that we could re-live the events of our wedding day. Two student nurses took great delight in looking at these photographs, and later two staff nurses did the same. It was a joy to share our happiness with them. It probably amused them to see men with long sideburns and women wearing the styles of a bygone age. It was a happy and positive day.

Eileen had a lot of visitors the next day to prepare her for her discharge, and this left her feeling tired.

On Friday morning, various aids were delivered to our house. It felt good to be going to the hospital not just for the regular visit but in order to take Eileen home. There were some emotional farewells, for Eileen had made a big impression on others in her ward.

6
L-PLATE CARER

It felt good to see Eileen sitting in her easy chair again, with its splendid view of the sea. This was where she belonged. In my worst moments I had imagined that she would never sit there again. She retired to bed early. It took me a while to adjust the pillows: I had a lot to learn.

After breakfast on Saturday morning, I returned to bed, and we talked together about what God was doing in Eileen's life at this time. As a carer, I would face limitations which might take some getting used to. Eileen stayed in bed till the middle of the day, and then had a leisurely bath. I had to help her getting in and out of the bath-tub. She had lost over two stones in weight, and I aimed to provide good food so that she put put this weight back on again. All through her life she had been trying to lose weight. Now, ironically, it was just the opposite. That day she sought to help me make the evening meal, but, in doing so, overtired herself. I was going to have to get used to the kitchen being primarily my realm rather than Eileen's. This would be hard for us both. On this and successive days she would retire to bed around 9. I would undress and lie with her for a while; then I would go downstairs to read for an hour or so. With the exception of the bath, this would be our daily routine.

The congregation at Kircubbin on Sunday gave me a lovely spray of flowers to take back for Eileen. I was told about pastoral visits that needed to be made, but I did not know whether I would have opportunity to follow these up properly. That evening there was a combined Anglican and Presbyterian service at Greyabbey. This was not the interdenominational service that we were planning for a later date, but it was a good start. The Presbyterian minister, Mark, led the worship and I preached. There was a warm atmosphere.

I became conscious on Monday of the many extra things that would need to be done to make Eileen's life comfortable. Today this included receiving the district nurse, welcoming visitors and performing various domestic tasks. Eileen was able to eat only small portions: it became obvious that helping her put on weight was going to be a real challenge. Disappointed to hear that Eileen could not be fitted into this week's oncology clinic, I wrote in the journal: *"These are very difficult days, and we are so much in need of the Lord's help"*.

Eileen was very sick some time after 1am, but, after some medication, got off to sleep again. I arranged for the doctor to make a house call. I wrote:

> *"Sitting in my recliner, I reflected that Jesus was in control even when it did not look like it, the Father would be glorified whatever our circumstances and the Spirit would take my poor prayers and make them into powerful and effective ones."*

On Wednesday I drove to the airport to pick up Eileen's friends Kath and Chris, from her old Wolverhampton women's group, who had flown over just for the day. Because of heavy traffic, I was delayed. They had come primarily to see Eileen, but I knew that if they spent the whole day with her it would make her very tired. Diplomacy was needed. (Another gift for good carers!) I therefore included in their visit a walk round the local area and a drive round parts of the Ards peninsula, so that Eileen could have periods of rest. On the return journey in the dark, I drove over a grass verge when turning into the airport, and, judging by their startled manner, I think they must have been glad that I was not taking them any further.

*

In January we were required to spend a fortnight at Crowther Hall, a part of the Selly Oak colleges in Birmingham, so that Eileen could learn more about CMS and feel that she was a part of the family. The small room which we occupied was up a few steps, with 'his' and 'hers' toilets on either side. The cold, snowy weather kept us indoors a lot, and it is thus not surprising that it was during this period that our first child was conceived.

*

At this time, Eileen found that sitting a lot made her uncomfortable. I discovered that there was a shop in Comber which sold goods for people who were in any way disabled, and this included foam rings. After I had made a special journey to buy one for the princely sum of £20; it proved to be not very helpful, and shortly afterwards we got an air cushion free of charge from Occupational Therapy.

On Sunday morning, before I scraped the ice off the car windows in order to get to church, Eileen said she would prefer an early death to a long life as an invalid. Neither of these options sounded attractive: there was ice in my soul as well.

It was good that my responsibilities at Greyabbey and Kircubbin were winding down just at a time when caring for Eileen was the main priority. I expected that I would be preaching that day for the last time at Greyabbey and Kircubbin. What I did not then know was that, because of the sheer impossibility of the new Rector getting to three services on a Sunday morning, I would still be preaching fortnightly at Greyabbey. The next day I made my farewell pastoral visits. At least, there would be closure here. I thanked the Lord for his good timing.

The evening before our next appointment at the hospital, we made a list of questions we wanted to ask. On the day itself we had to drive through the rush hour. On arrival we asked for a hospital wheelchair, and this involved a wait of 20 minutes. My anxiety level was rising; but I need not have worried, for we were not called till 90 minutes after the appointed time. Dr. McKenna was a slightly built woman, who looked too young to have all the specialist knowledge which she obviously had. She appeared to have a genuine concern for our needs. "The cancer can be brought under control," she told us, "but not eradicated." She explained too that it was most unusual for two unrelated types of cancer – lymphatic and ovarian - to attack the body at the same time. Treatment was likely to begin on Monday week. There would be a separate cocktail of drugs for each condition. It was going to be a difficult time, but, if it gave Eileen a better quality of life, it was worth it.

When we got home, we found that a wheelchair and an inflatable mattress and cushion had been delivered in our absence. Sandra, a district nurse, came and showed us how to inflate them. Tired because of such an early start, Eileen wanted to go to bed early. The new mattress should allow her to lie more comfortably. I was getting used to helping Eileen to arrange the pillows properly.

I came to value that hour in the evening just before bed when I could sit with a book. There was still some warmth left from the coal and log fire which I had prepared earlier. For a while I could forget the pressures of being a carer and just have time to myself. I called this my 'me-time', and this was one of the keys to survival. The weekly trip to the supermarket was also a kind of 'me-time'. Although it was a chore that had to be done, it was an excursion away from the house, and I learned to take pleasure in it. This was also a store which Eileen and I had not visited together.

I did another bit of shopping when Eileen said she would enjoy some delicacies from Marks and Spencer's but I was surprised to find the place heaving with people. That was because, for that day only, there was a reduction of 20% off many goods. I had chosen a busy day.

On the afternoon of that day, I took Eileen out for her first 'walk' in the wheelchair. She was not ashamed to be seen by the neighbours in this condition. It gave me the opportunity to explore which parts of our neighbourhood were most wheelchair-friendly. The birds were in good form: we saw two redshanks in the lagoon area, a diving cormorant, a cluster of oystercatchers and a group of brent geese feeding on the grass.

I had a dilemma one evening. I had been invited to the induction of Gill Withers as Rector of the Greyabbey group of churches, but to attend would mean leaving Eileen alone. We both agreed that I should go. After a long service, we all went to Rosemount, home of the Montgomery family, for refreshments. As this time was drawing to a close, the Bishop spoke of Eileen's vision for the peninsula and led us all in prayers for her health. People in my vicinity laid hands on me, as a substitute for Eileen herself. I could not wait to get home so that I could share this with Eileen.

We both continued to be sustained by our times of prayer and Bible Study. At this time I felt God was saying to me, "I want you to trust me in your time of trouble, so I can rescue you, and you can give me glory." What form would that rescue take?

*

Before our return to Taiwan, we had some deputation ministry in Ireland. In Dublin we attended a Communion service at which the Archbishop of Dublin was celebrant; and this was followed by a 'Meet the Missionaries' session. In the question time that followed our talk, one woman asked me about the bloodthirsty passages in the Old Testament – not the sort of question one was used to fielding on such occasions. We also attended a meeting of the Dublin University Far East Mission. Historically, they had been linked with Fuchien province on the Mainland of China; but this was the time of the Cultural Revolution, and the best they could do for the time being was to forge links with Taiwan.

When we arrived back in Belfast, rioting was taking place. We heard the cries of young people and the crack of rubber bullets. Through the window we saw youths pushing a van along the road, probably to form part of a barricade. It was all so pointless. Even when we were being driven to the airport, we had to take a roundabout route because of a bomb scare.

*

There were several new developments. A man came to fix a new stair rail. A Macmillan nurse came to give Eileen advice about medicines. This was timely, as she was not having a very good day. There was also a telephone call from Dr. McKenna, asking Eileen to go to the hospital on Wednesday for tests on the kidneys to ensure that they would be able to process the toxic waste effectively after each dose of chemotherapy.

It was still proving very difficult to help Eileen gain weight. She ate little and often, and even then she would sometimes bring it back. I could have felt guilty about failing in my attempts, but I knew I was working against great odds.

There was nothing, however, wrong with my own appetite. I left her alone on one other occasion in order to attend a pensioners' Christmas lunch at Rubane. I had a good excuse to return home when the rest of them were occupied with dancing.

On some days, Eileen felt very tired, and spent a lot of her time sleeping. This was so different from the vibrant wife with whom I had lived all those years.

It was time once again to send out our Christmas prayer letters. This would reach a much wider circle than the e-mails we sent out every so often about Eileen's health. I believe that Eileen's peace and my own strength were given as an answer to prayer. We each received the very gift we needed for our situation.

I left Eileen alone again for a short time in order to enjoy an early Christmas dinner with local clergy. (Some more 'me-time'.) As I ate heartily, I wished that Eileen could have done the same.

46

Our next visit to the hospital was postponed from Wednesday to Friday. The Bridgewater Suite, though in the main hospital rather than in the cancer hospital, was set up for the treatment of cancer patients. It was tastefully designed. There were several areas to sit. Those who wanted to watch television could use a special room; others, who chose not to do so, could read the day's newspaper or simply chat. Free hot drinks and biscuits were on hand throughout the day. On this visit, Eileen was to have a series of blood tests at ever widening intervals. At first she was in a large shared room; but when the staff saw how tired she was, they found her a private room, where she could rest on a bed. What could have been a stressful day, therefore, proved in the end to be restful. We were given soup and sandwiches at lunch time and I was even given a permit for free parking. It worried me to see Eileen moving about so slowly and painfully, a mere shadow of her former self. She had never been an invalid, despite having her fair share of illnesses, and this was not the sort of life we would have chosen for her.

*

In the middle of February it was time for us to return to Taiwan to set up home together for the first time. On the way we spent a few days in Singapore, staying with friends. There we did some shopping, visited the OMF headquarters, explored the Botanical Gardens and called on other friends.

The next stage of the journey took us back to Hong Kong. This time we stayed with Joyce Bennett of CMS at St. Catherine's School for Girls. She would become the first British Anglican woman to be ordained. We met Mr. Chu, whose name had been suggested as the official photographer for CMS's forthcoming Taiwan project. We also met Mrs. Dunn of OMF who had rescued us the last time we were passing through the colony.

Toward the end of our short stay, Eileen coughed a lot and felt sick. She remained like that on the ongoing flight to Taiwan. At the airport we were met by Bishop Pong and his right hand man, Dr. Lei and some of our personal friends. That evening the Bishop and his wife, together with Dr. Lei and myself, went for a meal in a restaurant, but Eileen was not well enough to join us.

Somehow Eileen got through the train journey on the next day. On our arrival at the station, there were several students from the hostel and some Western friends waiting to greet us. The students had arranged a welcome meeting; but Eileen had to retire to bed at the home of our friends, the Craighills, with whom we would stay until our own home was ready.

*

Eileen came to rely more and more on what the Lord had taught me for her own spiritual nourishment, Those long periods of sitting in an easy chair in the bedroom poring over the Word were over. On the 14th we prayed that God would honour his promise to be a 'place of safety' for us; but it was not an easy day. Eileen was feeling very nauseous and could not eat her food. I stayed at home with her instead of going to church. We phoned the emergency doctor, and he came to give her an anti-sickness jab. After this she slept most of the time.

*

During the next day at the Craighills', Eileen was still in a lot of discomfort. Our friend, Dr. Shao, was kind enough to take us in his car to the Father Fox Hospital, where she was accepted as an in-patient. She was there for a few days, while they sought to deal with the mucus that hindered her breathing. It was established that she had pneumonia. This was not the best introduction to our new life together in Taiwan. I looked forward to the day when she would be fit to move to the Japanese bungalow, where she would take up her role as mistress of the house.

*

The following day we went back to the Bridgewater Suite for an assessment prior to chemotherapy. First of all, as standard procedure, there was a blood test. We then spent some time with the consultant, Dr. McKenna. She asked a lot of questions, and told us that she hoped not only to give her chemotherapy but also to improve her physical condition. This could be better achieved if Eileen were to become an in-patient for a little while.

Eileen was lying on a bed, waiting for a place on a ward, when I left her to go home for her things. When I returned, she was on Ward 2 of the Cancer Hospital, in a private room with ensuite facilities. As she had a sudden attack of diarrhoea while I was there, we were grateful for this privacy. For a short

48

time, I would not be her daily carer, but would rest assured that she was getting good care round the clock from the experts.

7
COCKTAILS IN THE SUITE

Up to this time I was very ignorant about chemotherapy. I knew, of course, that it was used to kill off malignant cells, but that was the extent of my knowledge. The thought of such treatment, like the cancer itself, scares many people.

For us, the start of chemotherapy was a sign of hope. After a long period of investigation, at last something was being done to try to put things right. It was therefore with a sense of relief and anticipation that we prepared for the first course of treatment.

One thing I had not been aware of before was that the treatment is matched to the nature of the disease and the capacity for treatment in each patient. It is administered only after a blood test has been administered. From such tests a wealth of information can be gleaned. What is prepared for the patient is a cocktail of chemicals, and the strength given also varies according to the condition of the patient. As Eileen had two kinds of cancer, there were two different cocktails of chemicals that she was to be given. On the first day each time she would receive carboplatin. There was talk of adding another chemical, somewhat more severe and causing hair loss, which would have given a 10% better chance of success; but it was felt that she was too frail to take this. On the second day she would be given retuximab. This would happen six times at three week intervals.

When I visited Eileen in hospital, I found she had been moved to Ward 1, and had a room to herself. There was also a large plasma television set on the wall, the gift of a kind donor, but we had scarcely any use for that. Some patients would have watched it all the time. Her anti-sickness medication was effective, but it made her more tired.

The following day the treatment began. The carboplatin was in a brown bag, and the contents would slide down a tube into the patient's body. It was a slow process, and the patient was quite free to chat or to read, or even to doze. In our case, the machine kept stopping, and nurses had to keep coming in to fix it. A display of figures on the machine indicated how much of the drug had already been administered. When a bag became empty, the machine would emit a little jingle, which became monotonous after a while.

The day after this, Eileen had her first dose of retuximab. I could not get my tongue round these unfamiliar words at first, but before long they were as much a part of the vocabulary as 'cup of tea' or 'sandwich'.

There were no side effects that were immediately obvious. Eileen felt tired, but she had already been tired before the treatment began. Nausea, another side effect, was also something with which she was already familiar.

Others who have had a course of chemotherapy usually find that there is not much effect after the first dosage, but that the effect is cumulative as the treatment continues. Even so, the effects vary from person to person. During such a course, it is important to try to stay away from any source of infection, as the results could be worse than under normal circumstances. After all, the chemicals are killing not only fast-growing cancer cells but also some cells that are not cancerous, thus leaving the system more vulnerable to disease.

When I saw Eileen the following day, a woman came to talk with her about palliative care. We also had a visit from an occupational therapist. An unexpected side effect at this stage was itchiness, but some medication was provided for this. The main thing, as far as we were concerned, was that treatment had begun, and with it, hopefully, the process of healing.

*

It took a while to get the house as we wanted it. A new gas stove was fitted. Beds and a kitchen table had to be bought. The task of installing the water heater was much bigger than anticipated. Some painters came to smarten the place up. Our Bishop came with the Bishop of Honolulu to inspect the progress. We enjoyed opening our trunk and getting reacquainted with possessions from the UK. In the middle of it all came the dreadful news of a Baptist missionary who had been murdered by her cook.

The house was almost completely furnished. What we lacked was three things for our small square living room - a carpet, a cabinet and a fan. An American friend said he had some things to give away. Would we like them? Gratefully we accepted the offer. What were they? You have guessed it. And the carpet (which he called a 'rug') was exactly the right size. The Lord had measured it beforehand.

*

On Saturday evening I went to the airport to pick up Andrew, who had come over from Korea to spend Christmas with us. Jmin had been unable to make the journey. The next day we ate chili con carne together before going to see Eileen. Although I was not really up to that place yet, I read, in Andrew's presence, some words written just after his birth in 1973:

> *"Andrew, if ever you read this, know that your mother and I rejoiced in the supreme happiness of that moment. Know too that your middle name was chosen for its true meaning: you are indeed the gift of God to us. There were so many factors which could have prevented you from coming to us; but God overcame them all, and now we are a family of three, the creation of God."*

*

Our Christmas family was growing. The next morning I went to the airport to collect JoJoy. A little later in the day we went to the hospital to bring Eileen home. As the medication had not yet come from the pharmacy, we had to wait for nearly three hours. We amused ourselves by watching part of the film, "Finding Neverland".

That same evening, after supper, it was time to pick up Chris and Lauri from the airport. Now we were all ready to spend Christmas together. It was rather poignant, for there was a possibility that this would be the last Christmas we would all be able to share.

The following day, the 23rd, we bought in various Christmas goods, including the turkey we had ordered. When I took Eileen out in her wheelchair, it was dry and mild, but the sun was already failing. Our old friends, the oystercatchers and brent geese, were out in force to keep us company. I had been informed that I was to have a holiday from the kitchen, so it was Chris and Lauri who served up the sausage and mash for our evening meal.

We celebrated Christmas one day early, as JoJoy had to get back home. We opened our presents, therefore, mid-morning on the 24th. So many times in the past we had observed this ritual, and the floor would become a forest of discarded paper. Eileen and I were not allowed anywhere near the kitchen while the special dinner was being prepared. Our plates were piled high with food. (I have sometimes been tempted to go for a quiet Christmas with simple meals, but it would be hard to convince others.) Although Eileen had a smaller portion than the rest of us, she was able to get it down. To see her eating better was like a special Christmas gift. After the meal I took JoJoy back to the airport. On my return I was allowed back into the kitchen to strip the turkey.

On Christmas Day, when I attended the 9 o'clock Communion service at St. Patrick's, several people asked how Eileen was. Kevin, our minister, came to see Eileen when his services were over.

Our main meal, unsurprisingly, that evening was turkey pie; but Eileen could not keep it down. She looked somewhat wasted: the disease had robbed her not only of flesh but also strength.

Andrew, with his love of board games, persuaded us all to play 'Cranium' the next day, and we actually found ourselves unexpectedly enjoying it. When I drove Chris and Lauri to the airport, only Andrew then remained.

The rest of his stay soon passed. There was shopping to be done. Sunday, apart from church, was a lazy day. We enjoyed watching successive episodes of 'Yes Minister', a Christmas gift.

When I drove Andrew back to the airport on the 30th for the first stage of his journey back to Seoul, I could not help wondering whether he would ever see his mother alive again.

So, after a bitter-sweet family Christmas, we found ourselves alone again. I was learning to balance my role as carer with shopping, domestic duties, some writing and the watching of TV programmes together. Normally we would stay up till midnight to see the new year in. This year, for the first time, we went to bed earlier; but I was still lying there awake when the midnight chimes introduced the new year.

8

LIVING IN HOPE

Our next hospital appointment was on Friday the 2nd. We got to the hospital in 35 minutes, which was a record for us. Eileen had the usual blood test, and an hour later we saw Dr. Kettle, whose task it was to deal with the lymphoma. It was decided that in future the retuximab treatment which he had authorized would be given the day after the other treatment, at three weekly intervals. After this we saw very little of him: our other consultations were with Dr. McKenna or one of her deputies.

As the new Rector was responsible for three morning congregations, I had been asked to continue to take a service at Greyabbey on a fortnightly basis. When I turned up on the first Sunday of the year, there were many enquiries as to Eileen's health, and I could tell that this sprang from a genuine concern for both of us. At a time when my activities were so limited, I was glad to have this responsibility, and the Lord enabled me to carry out these duties perfectly normally, despite my personal circumstances. In fact, it was an opportunity to show others how it was possible to face great difficulties in God's strength. I was able to get back home before Eileen was ready to get up for the day.

The next day I had to get the title deeds to our house from the bank at Ballynahinch. I took Eileen with me so that she could visit her sister. I also went to the electrical shop, McCoubrey's, to order a flat-screen TV and a Freesat system so as to brighten up Eileen's world a little more. Although it cost a lot of money, the Lord had given us a healthier bank balance than we had had for a long time, and we could well afford it.

As I took down the Christmas decorations, I wondered whether Eileen would still be around to spend other Christmases with me.

*

Eileen's health gradually returned to normal. Now her thoughts were for maternity clothes, as she was growing in size. She was able to alter some of her current clothes, and friends brought other outfits for her to wear. As the days got hotter, it became uncomfortable for her. To be heavily pregnant during the hot summer days of Taiwan was not a good idea!

The next day, when I returned from a trip to Donaghadee, I found that Gregor was visiting Eileen. "I was delighted," he said, " that Eileen was able to open the door herself". He would continue to be a regular visitor. As for myself, I rarely travelled outside of Millisle, unless it was to keep a hospital appointment or to do the week's shopping. I wanted to be with Eileen as much as possible.

We discovered that we were not the only couple with mobility problems. Winston had his leg in plaster, which threw more responsibility on Betty for a time.

JoJoy said she had attended a conference for which we had originally booked ourselves. The speaker offered a powerful prayer for Eileen and spoke of others who had been healed, This gave Eileen new hope.

When I worshipped at St. Patrick's on Sunday, Kevin gave me some Communion bread to take back for Eileen, so that she might feel included.

On a mild and sunny Monday, we set out once again for the City Hospital. Our appointment this time was not until 1.30, so there was no rush. Eileen had the usual blood test. Instead of Dr. McKenna, we saw a Dr. Miller, who was in the later stages of pregnancy. She confirmed that we would use only carboplatin and not the severer drug. This way, there would be a 70% rather than an 80% chance of survival; but the odds still seemed good, and we also had prayer on our side.

We had some good news that day. Some time ago, Eileen had read about an initiative by Monty Don. He had arranged for disadvantaged young people to learn agriculture by working on allotments, and this had been a great success. She had been inspired to get a similar programme going in Millisle. The first step had been to lease a field from a local landowner and turn it into a garden. We had arranged the lease, but needed planning permission from the Council. This was a slow and weary process, but on this day we learned that permission had been granted. Now the work of transformation could begin.

Our next appointment at the hospital was on Wednesday. It was daunting to think of all this toxic material invading Eileen's body; but if it was going to kill the cancer cells it was worth it. We stayed long enough to receive our soup and sandwiches for lunch.

We had to return the next day for the retuximab. When it was discovered that the drug had not been ordered, there was a long delay. A place had been found for us in a side room with a bed, which made the situation more bearable. By the time we were able to get away, it was 5pm and we had to plough through the rush hour traffic.

When Eileen weighed herself, she discovered that she had put back six of the pounds that she had lost. I felt I must be doing something right! There were still days, however, when Eileen could not eat very much. On such days, I would have to throw good food away – something we had never done throughout our years together. The effect of the chemotherapy was also giving Eileen a 'dip' in her spirits.

It was, in fact, like a giant rollercoaster: there were up times and there were down times, times when hope burned bright and times when there did not seem a lot of hope.

Sometimes we claim as Christians that we have hope to carry us through. What, then, is the nature of that hope? Does it mean we can have confidence that we shall be healed? We know that God can heal, but the reality is that sometimes he does and sometimes he does not. On occasions a Christian may have a deep assurance that healing is going to take place, but that is far from a universal occurrence.

Our hope, then, lies chiefly in something beyond. It lies in the assurance that the God who was promised us salvation through Jesus Christ, will not go back on that promise. Not only are we saved from guilt now, but we shall enter into the presence of God as the completion of that salvation, in the life to come. Compared with all that, we shall consider that we have previously merely been creeping around in the shadows. It is the fulfilment of all that we have been made for. Moreover, God will by his grace keep us ready for that time and nothing, not even death, will separate us from the love of Christ.

What, then, about our marriage relationship? Shall we see our loved ones again? We are encouraged to believe that this will happen, but I also see a change of perspective. It is no longer a matter of gazing into each others' eyes, but rather of standing side by side as, together, we look into the face of God.

So our hope is all about what happens after death? Not entirely. We believe in God's keeping power in the present life. We believe that all works together for good to those who love God. We believe that this future hope gives us such strength to live out our present lives that we can give encouragement and hope to others. There is a purpose that runs all through this life and into the next. All this is the basis of any witness we are able to make while we are going through our trials.

There were still practical and temporal things to consider. I was persuaded to hire a woman called Lindsay to clean for us once a week. I knew I could do a good job myself, but here was opportunity to swallow my pride and lighten my own load a bit.

It was good to have visits from people who had meant a lot to us. Harry and Dorothy Smith came all the way from Rostrevor to see us. Mel and Carolyn arrived the same day for some ministry. This time they stayed at Betty's second house, just down the road from us, to save us from having to do a lot for them; but I made them some broth to give them a good Irish welcome. On the same day, Lindsay came to clean for the first time, and a district nurse came to visit. It seemed good for me to go to Tesco's while Lindsay was in the house.

The long awaited meeting of ministers from the Ards peninsula took place at Greyabbey. There were 11 of us. It was the beginning of the fulfilment of our vision. We shared about what God had done in each of our patches. I left early in order to look after Eileen, but not before they had begun to discuss plans for a united praise service.

After supper that day we read from the journal about a holiday at Yang Ming Shan.

*

Yang Ming Shan was a hilly area just to the north of Taipei. Occasionally there would be a winter snowfall, and crowds of local tourists would flock to see this unusual phenomenon. It was summer, however, when we went to the Ease Garden hostel for our holiday. The hostel was managed by a Chinese who liked to call himself 'Charlie Brown', though I don't think his mother would have known him by this name. The establishment boasted sulphur baths, which we made use of a few times. We ate the first day at the International Hotel, but it did not live up to its reputation when we saw a diner take out his teeth and wash them in a bowl. During the week we enjoyed good walks. We also swam at a pool, but Eileen felt self-conscious because of her size. On three occasions we ate at an American base, where the food was truly Western, and not a bland Chinese imitation. The weather was not uniformly good, but we had indoor places such as a museum to go to. We also dropped down into Taipei for some shopping and in order to visit old friends. It was our last holiday as a childless couple.

*

I took Eileen to Newtownards for an appointment with the plastic surgeon. He looked at the portion of the jaw from which the melanoma had been removed a few years earlier and pronounced that there would be no need for any more follow-up appointments.

On Friday I took Eileen to Ballynahinch to see Betty and her cast-bound husband. There would be no hiking for some time. I was the healthiest of the four. I also went back to McCoubrey's to chose a new Henry vacuum cleaner, as our old cleaner was giving us trouble. This one would be much easier to carry up and down the stairs.

On Saturday at Greyabbey I preached at the funeral of a man I had often visited in the past. Our fortunes were intertwined; for I had visited the couple at the Ards Community Hospital when he was an in-patient on the very day that Eileen's cancer was first discovered.

There was some amusement during the worship at St. Patrick's when Kevin, the Rector, produced a pair of scales and announced that he was undertaking a sponsored slim in aid of the rectory fund.

On Tuesday evening we ate with friends at the home of Declan and Peris Bowers. Declan was a former Roman Catholic priest, now a good Protestant Christian. His wife was an African who hailed from Kenya. It was Eileen's first social engagement since the start of her illness. After an ample meal, there was a time of prayer for Eileen, and also for Declan, who had a wasting disease that was probably neurological in origin.

When writing to our prayer partners I dared to suggest that Easter would be a sort of 'resurrection' time for us. Time would tell whether such a hope was justified.

The chairman and treasurer of our Community Association came to the house on Wednesday afternoon to fill in an application form for a further grant towards an event to launch the garden project. This meant than when an elderly couple came to see how Eileen was, I could not give them a lot of my attention.

On Friday we had to go to the City Hospital again for a blood transfusion. This meant that I would be unable to join with other members of the committee to meet the Minister for the Environment. We were glad that a single room was provided for us, as it was a long process. We had to wait a long time until the blood was ready; Eileen then had to receive two bags of blood at two hours a time. This transfusion put new strength into her. There is room for a sermon illustration here.

As the month came to an end, we were glad that Eileen's treatment was under way; but we recognized that anything was possible from the best to the worst scenario. Such uncertainty, even for people who claimed to live in hope, was hard to live with.

9
BEST FOOT FORWARD

It was a cold morning as I conducted worship at Greyabbey on the first day of February. The heating system was never very effective in that church. People would complain about my cold hands as we exchanged parting handshakes. Once again people asked about Eileen's health, and one lady gave us some organic goodies.

On Monday morning it was time to return to the City Hospital. Eileen was called very quickly for her blood test. Our consultant was Dr. Miller again: she told us it had been decided to keep Eileen on the one drug. She gave us some figures that indicated good progress; and this was another reason for avoiding the severer drug. We had to wait till 1 o'clock before the carboplatin was ready to be administered, but the process then only took half an hour. This time everything took place in a communal room rather than in a smaller room. Patients came in all shapes and sizes and age groups. Cancer does not just attack the elderly. Eileen felt that she had turned a corner, and was determined to work towards her complete rehabilitation.

Ice and snow had affected many parts of the UK; but the road to Belfast was clear as we made our way back to the hospital the next day for the retuximab. This time Eileen was able to relax in a room with a bed.

I discovered, when I took a document for signing to the chairman of our Community Association committee, another Roy, that his wife had fallen and broken her arm; and I sought to offer some sympathy.

In our readings from old journals, we had come to the story of Andrew's birth.

*

We had taken the train to Chang Hua simply for a check-up; but we were informed on arrival that the birth was imminent, and Eileen should prepare for admission. I had not brought any spare clothes with me. Eileen did not appreciate it when, as the pains were beginning, she was walking with me round the stalls, looking for a spare shirt. The birth process took several hours. While we were in the middle of this, a woman in street clothes appeared and climbed on to the next bed. Within minutes we heard the wail of a child.

She was obviously well used to this kind of thing. We sought to use the La Maze method, which we had been practising together. It was a great moment when Andrew's head first appeared, and I felt privileged to be there to witness it.

The next thing was to inform both sets of parents. At the telegraph office, I had to wake the boy up. In his confusion, he thought 'England' was the name of a town. After a long period of consulting his books, he managed to find my country under the initial 'P' – 'United Kingdom' in French! I had often wondered what lay behind the use of French in certain situations: if you wanted to send out a parcel from Taiwan, the forms were in Chinese and French; yet the country had never been a French possession, neither had it had many French inhabitants.

Eileen remained in Chang Hua for a few days while I returned to carry out my duties. A few days later I had the joy of escorting mother and child back to Tainan and showing off the new arrival to the students. Eileen would always speak proudly of that moment.

*

Our parish was about to start its mission week. A host of imaginative activities had been arranged. Under normal circumstances, Eileen and I would have been heavily involved, but these were not normal circumstances. However, I was able to attend the opening service at St. Patrick's, at which Bishop Harold spoke on 'love' and a man from Portadown gave his testimony.

On Monday morning, work began on the Community Garden. The dull, misty weather did not give us a brilliant start. The Conservation Volunteers arrived in two vans. Children came from the primary school to pick up the litter. A photographer from 'The Chronicle' came to record the event. It was a pity that Eileen could not be there personally. That evening the committee met again, but I had to leave early to help Eileen get to bed.

From time to time during her illness, Eileen was afflicted with constipation. One such attack had been countered by prayer, which meant that she was fit to travel to Ballynahinch to keep her hair appointment. While this was being done, I went back to McCoubrey's to order a digital recorder. I was becoming a good customer. The delivery date for this and the equipment ordered earlier

61

would be this coming Thursday. After a cup of tea with Winston and Betty, we travelled back, breaking our journey at Comber for a rare visit to the farm shop.

We enjoyed a visit from Kevin and Bishop Harold. They said that mission events up to this point had been well attended, and quite a number of people had put their trust in Christ.

As it was milder and sunnier on Thursday, I took Eileen out for a walk after lunch, using the wheelchair. It was a pleasant experience for us both, though birds on this occasion were few in number. Our new television equipment was installed the same day. I wondered about the expense, but it seemed right in that Eileen now spent so much of her time at home.

During this period, I tried to give Eileen as normal a life as possible. In many ways life was far from normal: we would not usually make all these hospital visits, take trips in wheelchairs, spend so much time in bed or dozing in a chair, go through a detailed regimen of medicines, excuse ourselves from attending meetings and so on. At the same time, there were some normal activities that were still possible. We loved to 'walk' along the coast, examining the scenery and the wildlife; we loved to reflect on things we had done in the past, we loved to watch our favourite programmes such as 'Lark Rise to Candleford', we loved to read good books, we also enjoyed playing Scrabble; when, on occasions, we could visit a sister or a friend, or go to a shop, that was a bonus. I felt it was important that Eileen should be involved in as much 'normal' activity as she was able to take in her condition.

Even getting to church, once a very normal activity, had become only an occasional affair. On the Thursday of the mission we went to Carrowdore for a healing service. It was the first time Eileen had attended a worship service since October. A team from Belfast came and prayed the same short prayer for anyone who requested it. After the service, Eileen asked the leader, David, to pray for her personally. Although it meant she got to bed later than usual, she seemed none the worse for this.

I attended a 'dads and lads' breakfast on Saturday morning as part of the mission. Before the meal some of us played a virtual reality game that involved ski jumping. It is just as well it was not the real thing, for I did not make a very good job of it. After the meal, a missioner called Roger gave an evangelistic address.

At Greyabbey on Sunday morning I preached on 'the sovereignty of Christ'. Once again, people expressed their concern for Eileen and I came away with some beautiful flowers for her. That afternoon, Eileen did not feel like going for a walk or attending 'Songs of Praise 'at Carrowdore, and it worried her that this should be so.

Watching 'The Antiques Road Show' and 'Lark Rise to Candelford' in HD for the first time was almost as good as being there in person. We had come a long way since the days of those old flickering black and white sets.

There was one sign of progress: Eileen no longer needed toilet seats for the disabled. It was with great pleasure that I took them back to the depot in Bangor. I hoped that other aids would soon be able to be returned also.

On Wednesday I drove Eileen to Donaghadee for afternoon tea at the Cafe Manor. This was another attempt at a 'normal' activity. With her Irish blood, Eileen was very fond of coffee shops. After this refreshment, she was able to walk with me to a shoe shop to buy some slippers. The whole experience did a lot for our sense of wellbeing.

While I was cleaning the car, I noticed that the new seal sculptures that we had commissioned were being put in place on the grassy area of the car park behind our house. This was yet another of the improvements that we were making to the locality. One passer-by remarked that it was a waste of money; but this was the only negative comment I ever heard. Children sprawled across them, weary travellers sat on them, and keen photographers made a pictorial record of them.

On Friday morning we went for a blood test to prepare Eileen for Monday. Later in the morning we drove into Bangor. Eileen was able to walk with me from the car park to the solicitor's office so that we could update our wills. Eileen was particularly anxious that the contents of her savings account, in the event of her death, should be shared between our sons. We waited in a large and cluttered Dickensian office, where two secretaries were at work, until our appointment could take place.

At this time, I felt that God was using my current experiences to change me and to make me more like himself. In God's good economy, nothing is wasted.

On Saturday Eileen and I took a walk round the car park without recourse to a wheelchair. It felt as if we were really making progress.

I made a rare visit to St. Patrick's for the Sunday morning service. In the past, Eileen would keep me in touch with the affairs of our local church through her regular attendance: now it was only through my occasional visits and through talks with Kevin that I was able to keep up with the news. The same afternoon we had a slightly longer walk via the lagoon. It was still much shorter than the old walks, but it was a good beginning.

*

A few days after bringing our new baby home from hospital, Eileen was out with the pram when she met a church member.

As people do, the lady inspected the new arrival and asked, "How old is he?"

"Just about a week", Eileen replied.

Immediately, the woman's face changed. It was a local tradition that a new baby and its mother should remain indoors for the first month. All this was highly irregular! She urged Eileen to return home immediately.

*

We made a very early start for the hospital on Monday morning. It was to our surprise that we had been informed by telephone that Eileen would be receiving the severer drug after all; but the consultant, now even more heavily pregnant, informed us that this was the work of an over-zealous staff nurse, and that there had been no change of plan. She was delighted to see Eileen walk into her consulting room for the first time instead of coming in on wheels. After the drug had been administered, we stayed for lunch.

At the AGM of our Community Association, our Chairman spoke of good things that had happened during the year. In the first phase of the Pharmacy Project, Eileen had organized some relaxation classes that included foot massage, and this had been much appreciated. Now Alana, the pharmacist, said that a grant had been applied for so that a second and more comprehensive stage of the project could begin. Sadly, this would be without Eileen.

64

The next day it took just an hour and a half to give Eileen the retuximab; but, because of waiting around, we were there for four hours. I slipped out to visit the bank, and found myself buying salami for a pushy Indian woman, who was selling 'The Big Issue'.

On this Ash Wednesday, I did not attend worship. This was because the service was at 11am, just when Eileen would be getting up. However, I was very conscious of the Lord's presence with me, and did not feel that he held it against me. In our own times of prayer together during Lent, we were praying for the persecuted Church.

A friend called me on Skype from Cyprus. He told me that Eileen had been prayed for in the local church. It was good to know that people in Australia, Japan, Indonesia, China, Canada, the USA and other parts of the world were praying for her.

When the district nurse came on her weekly visit, she was very pleased with Eileen's progress. This was the most upbeat period since the illness had first taken effect in the autumn.

On Friday there was a photo-shoot in the Community Garden with our MP, Lady Sylvia Hermon. It was a mild and sunny day – perfect for the occasion. The volunteers had already made some paths, and she was photographed planting a small tree in the central bed. It was good, after such a long wait, to see the project taking shape.

When our bank statement arrived, we discovered that two large sums of money had been placed in our account, and that we had over £10,000. Eileen had applied for a benefit that we had not claimed when the children were small, and, to our surprise, not only was the application successful, but the award was much greater than expected. This meant that, whatever uncertainties we faced in our immediate future, there would be no financial worries. This, in the middle of a recession, was good news indeed. The Lord's timing was so good.

We heard that it was likely that the Christian Renewal Centre at Rostrevor would close down in the coming year. Having been involved with the place almost since its inception, we were saddened at this news. However, God sometimes raises up an institution to meet a particular need at a particular time; and when that need has been met, there is no strong reason to prolong its life. Maybe that applies to us as individuals too. God has a particular work for each one of us. When we have achieved what he wanted us to do, there is no reason why our life on this earth should be further prolonged. Was this a lesson for us at this time?

The situation just then, however, was much more positive. Eileen was making good progress, and we had reason to believe that life would gradually become much more normal. In fact, when I told the Greyabbey congregation on Sunday that Eileen was now able to go for short walks with me, they broke into spontaneous applause.

10
NEW HORIZONS?

At the start of the new month there were several trips we made together which suggested that life was opening out for us again. The first of these was an evening meal with all the members of our Antioch Group at the home of our friends Teri and Jan. Over a delicious meal, we talked mainly about marriage relationships, as two of the couple had been attending a course. Eileen and I felt that God had greatly blessed our own marriage. If anything, our current trials had brought us even closer together.

Eileen resumed her patchwork after a long gap. She could not get to her class, but she could do the work at home. We also paid another visit to Betty's house in Ballynahinch and bought goods from the farm shop on the way back. In addition to all this, we paid a second visit to the solicitor's in Bangor in order to sign our wills and to give our sons power of attorney in case we should not be in a position to make decisions ourselves.

All, however, was not unmitigated progress. Eileen began to feel more tired, and her temperature was higher than usual. For myself, I was going through a period of toothache – an occasional affliction which no dentist had been able to deal with satisfactorily. After a couple of days, Eileen's energy was coming back and she was able to resume her patchwork. In fact, on Sunday she was able to help me prepare the lunch and even strip the chicken afterwards. It was as if I was getting the old Eileen back again.

Some time earlier, my old friends from Taiwan, Wilfred and Lily Chee, now living in Australia, had told me that they were about to visit the UK and would like to come and see me. I did not feel that Eileen's condition was an impediment to their visit, so I offered them a warm welcome. Ironically, they lived in that very suburb of Sydney, Eastwood, where Eileen and I had stayed during a holiday a few years earlier, and at that time we had not known they were there!

Aware that long exposure to visitors would make Eileen tired, I took them on a tour of the peninsula that first afternoon. For the evening meal I prepared lamb roast and plum crumble. Together we looked through our old photographs of Taipei and Tainan.

The next morning I took our guests for a walk round the immediate area. For lunch all four of us went to the Cafe Manor in Donaghadee. It was very much in the tradition of the Irish 'coffee shop', and our guests were impressed. That afternoon I took them to Bangor to see the harbour. We did a walkabout in Groomsport, where terns had seized control of their little island and were very vocal about it. They also showed me the house, just outside Donaghadee, where their daughter sometimes spent her holidays. It made the world seem rather small.

Wilfred and Lily took a bus into Belfast the next day, as they wanted to explore this rejuvenated city. I decided it was better to stay at home with Eileen. When they came back, I produced a pork casserole and they supplied rich desserts which they had bought from Marks and Spencer's.

The next morning I took them to the airport. Because of a road accident we were severely held up, and it was a bit of a cliffhanger. I was grateful to the Lord for giving me strength during their visit to look after them.

Eileen had yet another social engagement when the Antioch Group met for a meal at the home of David and Dorothy. What began as a prayer group seemed to have turned into a dining club. Each of our four families had been under attack, as if the devil did not like to have people praying for our area.

I cooked another good meal for our Sunday lunch. Afterwards Eileen spent a lot of time sleeping. It saddened me to see one who had so many gifts and abilities spending so much of her time inactive because of illness, whilst so many people who just idled their lives away sat around in perfect health. It was the old situation described in Psalm 73 – a passage I had often used when ministering to the sick and elderly. The Psalmist has exactly the same problem. God seems so unjust in his dealings. This man agonized about the problem until he drew closer to God and got his answer:

"Yet I am always with you;
you hold me by my right hand.
You guide me with your counsel.
And afterwards you will take me into glory.
Whom have I in heaven but you?
And being with you, I desire nothing on earth.
My flesh and my heart may fail,
but God is the strength of my heart
and my portion for ever."

We may have great wealth, many possessions and impeccable health; but if we do not have God we are paupers. It is our fellowship with God in this .life and the next that gives meaning to everything. So when I saw Eileen in this condition, it was our common knowledge of God that held everything together.

On Monday it was time for another visit to the hospital. We got there so early that we had to wait for reception to open. The consultant whom we saw this time was an Asian woman whom we had not met previously. She said that Eileen's current tiredness was due to a low haemoglobin count, and suggested another blood transfusion later in the week. We had to wait a long time until the drug was ready.

On St. Patrick's Day I would normally have joined in the pilgrimage from Saul to Downpatrick; but on this occasion I stayed at home without any tinge of guilt. We had a diet of television programmes and word games. It was good that we had similar tastes.

Because of the holiday, our second visit was on Wednesday instead of Tuesday. It was a mild and sunny day – the sort of weather when we would like to have been exploring out of doors. Later in the day, Lindsay brought her friend Kerry, who would do the cleaning for us in future.

I had not realized that blood transfusions could be given at home. A nurse came on Friday morning to begin the process, and she was replaced by a colleague around lunch time. This second nurse proved to be a devout Christian. These transfusions made Eileen feel stronger; and we felt grateful to the kind donors who had made this possible.

The first day of Spring was sunny, but it was rather cool; so Eileen felt she should stay indoors. Unusually for us, we watched the Ireland v Wales rugby match in which Ireland completed the Grand Slam.

On Mothering Sunday I attended the Family Service at St. Patrick's. It was sad to be there without Eileen. To Eileen's great pleasure, some beautiful flowers, which Andrew and Jmin had ordered from Korea, were delivered to her, and we also had opportunity to talk with both sons on the telephone. At this stage, the chemotherapy made Eileen very sleepy. However, we managed to listen to a talk about Charles Spurgeon. This was part of a set of talks given by John Piper on 'great Christian leaders'.

One thing I had not realized about Spurgeon was that, as well as being a great preacher and a staunch critic of Anglicanism, he also suffered a lot. His wife was an invalid for 27 years, and he himself suffered from gout, rheumatism and Brights Disease, as well as being the target for much ridicule and slander throughout his ministry. Charles Simeon suffered intense opposition when he first started his ministry at Holy Trinity, Cambridge; after 25 years of ministry his health suddenly failed, and often he could only speak in a whisper, but after 13 years he was suddenly healed. Jonathan Edwards, whom God used in times of revival, describes how he was taken ill at New Haven on the way home from a preaching trip, and had to stay there for 3 months; but that God was very close to him during this long illness. John Owen, the Puritan preacher, lost most of his children in their youth. George Whitefield, preacher during times of revival, was often so unwell that he could hardly stand up to preach, yet he could address 50,000 people in the open air without a microphone and still be heard. The upshot of all this is that often, when God wants to use a person, he allows him to go through suffering. Such suffering enriches him and gives him a more powerful ministry.

Should we, then, ask to be spared suffering? After all, the one who suffered the most was Jesus Christ himself. Any suffering which Eileen and I may have experienced is infinitely small compared with his, and yet, in our limited sense, we have been able to reach out to others and do some good in God's world.

Many of our days were purely routine. We still followed our customs of praying together and reading from the journal. Eileen's eyesight was deteriorating, as she was due to have cataracts removed, which meant that she could not do a lot of reading for herself.

*

For our first Christmas dinner as a little family, we had an unexpected guest – a young man called Randy who came from San Francisco. Like so many people during our time in Taiwan, he turned up out of the blue, occupied our guest bed, and then disappeared again. So many people like Randy appear as names in the journal, but we have no personal recollection of what they were like.

*

As Eileen's health was slowly improving, we began to make tentative plans for the future. Long distance holidays were, of course, out of the question, but we contemplated a trip with Ulsterbus round Killarney in the late summer. It was good to be able to look beyond the limitations enforced upon us at that time. For the time being, however, Eileen's tiredness precluded even going for short walks or other outings. The big events of the day would be the visit of a coalman or an electrician.

I still had opportunity to attend the occasional function on my own – a kind of extension of my 'me-time'. I had a meeting at Stormont, the splendid Northern Ireland parliament building, on the subject of 'neighbourhood renewal'. Everyone but myself seemed to be well versed in the subject. I did not find it easy to relate to others: maybe it was because I spent so much time quietly at home that I was getting unused to being in company.

That same evening I attended a Spring Fest at the Somme Centre. It was a gathering organized by the Council to thank people who gave voluntary service to their local communities. This was a happy and festive occasion, but I could not help thinking of poor Eileen, alone at home.

Wilson, the OMF regional director, came to see us, bringing the news that Elsie, a friend of Eileen's who had also served with the mission, had suffered a recurrence of the cancer for which she had been treated a few years earlier.

An early Communion service had been arranged at our local church; but when I went there I found it had been cancelled. After lunch Eileen and I celebrated Communion together, just the two of us.

On Monday it was milder, with a hazy sun, and Eileen felt well enough to take a short walk.

It was good to meet with other clergy on Tuesday to make plans for Pentecost Praise; even though I had to leave early to look after Eileen. Our vision was bearing fruit. We enjoyed another short walk together that same afternoon. It really looked as if we were facing newer, brighter horizons.

11
RESURRECTION IS CANCELLED

We had really been looking forward to April. It was to be our 'resurrection time'. The chemotherapy would come to an end; and our lives would gradually return to something like normal. The fact that all this would happen around Easter seemed like a happy coincidence.

When I was taking my morning jog, the sun came over the horizon as a big red ball. It was awesome. Over the years we had both come to appreciate greatly the beauty of the natural world. Gradually we had got to know the names of birds that we saw. Eileen loved to trace the various pastel shades of the sky as she sat in her easy chair, looking out of the window. Throughout this time of illness, with all the limitations that it brought, it was still possible for us to enjoy the natural world and to see God's hand in it all.

The next day, as Eileen had a pain in the femur, we rang the local surgery. At first we could not get an appointment, but when we rang again there had just been a cancellation. Our GP said it was likely to be arthritis, but suggested we go to Newtownards for an X-ray to check it out. We went straight there. The results could not be given immediately.

When I got back from the shopping, I found that our friend Elsie was visiting us. Although she was about to face major treatment for her own cancer, she still spared the time and trouble to visit us. I prepared a meal for all three of us.

Eileen was well enough the next day to go on another outing. We went to Marks and Spencer's to spend a voucher which Andrew and Jmin had given her, using the wheelchair, as it would have been too tiring for Eileen to walk round the store. She chose some dark trousers and two tops. It was a venture of faith, for this inferred that she would have plenty of opportunity to wear them. We also took afternoon tea in the coffee shop. I was so glad that Eileen was able to enjoy this before the effects of the final dose of chemotherapy set in.

We had a Sunday afternoon visit from Betty's son, Peter, and his fiancee, Sara. Their wedding was to take place in December. We hoped that Eileen would be well enough by then to travel to Edinburgh for this.

On Monday we went back to the Bridgewater Suite. As this was to be the last appointment of the course, we saw Dr. McKenna herself. She said she was pleased with the progress Eileen had been making and invited questions. We had to wait a long time for the treatment, but Eileen made good use of the bed provided, and slept most of the time. Although it was a long day away from home, Eileen was in good form.

At the committee meeting of our Community Association that same evening, our pharmacist gave us an update on how the Pharmacy Project was developing. The first phase had comprised Eileen's relaxation classes. Now it was possible to build on what Eileen had started to enter the second and much more varied stage.

The following day, we went back to the hospital for Eileen's last dose of retuximab. As she had her treatment, a man who originally came from Durham proved very talkative. The treatment finished around 2, and we were free to go home.

As we walked down the corridor, however, Eileen clutched me more tightly, for it was proving difficult to walk because of a pain. We took the lift to the ground floor. As we stepped out of the lift, there was a snap, and Eileen's leg gave way. Since we were just next to the snack bar, I was able to grab a chair and seat her on it. I asked a doctor to see her, and he arranged for her to go to the A&E department. The one positive feature was that this had happened about 80 yards from that department and not in some distant place. She was sent for an X-ray, which confirmed she had a broken femur. It was the effect of the cancer in her bones. She would need to be admitted to the Royal Victoria Hospital for an operation, as the City Hospital did not handle that sort of thing. I stayed with Eileen until she had received morphine to control the pain; and then I drove home to collect her things.

I remained at home for half an hour – just long enough to contact family and get myself something to eat. I then drove straight to the Royal, expecting that Eileen would already have been transferred. I was directed to the ward and even to the bedspace that she would occupy, but the ambulance had not yet brought her. I arrived at quarter to eight, but, because of the long wait for an ambulance, Eileen did not appear till around 10.50. I sat there feeling very uptight. Here we were in this severe and unexpected emergency, and we could not even be together. It was the nadir point of the whole process of the illness up till then. Our hopes of 'resurrection' had gone. It would take a long time for Eileen to regain her mobility. Up to this time, all things were possible – even a complete recovery. Now all this was changed, and we had to prepare ourselves

73

for the real possibility that the illness would be terminal. It was a watershed, and I had those three long hours to reflect upon it as I sat in solitude.

It was a great relief to me when Eileen was at last brought on to the ward. She was placed in a bay already occupied by three men. A young lady doctor took down her details and gave her more morphine. I thought that Eileen was bearing up much better than I was, for I was a nervous wreck, but she was still at peace. I left her at 12.15, and, in my confusion, drove home by an unintentionally roundabout route.

I had some practical tasks to do in the morning before catching buses to the Royal. I lunched in the hospital restaurant before going to see her. As this was not a cancer hospital, I would have to keep to strict visiting times. When I arrived, Eileen was away at the X-ray department, but she was soon back again. It was a matter of making her as comfortable as possible in preparation for surgery on the morrow. She had been put on a catheter. We had a quiet and relaxed time together.

The next morning Eileen called me to tell me that her operation had been postponed. How we valued our mobile phones during those difficult days! For years I had stood out against getting one, but it had now become an important lifeline. It would have been hard to survive without this facility.

That day my bus to town was delayed, with the result that I missed the hospital bus by 20 seconds. Although this simply meant a wait of half and hour (or a walk), I felt immensely frustrated, as this came on top of my other emotions, and I took a pointless punch at the bus shelter.

When I got to Eileen, we talked and read from the journal. I found it hard to accept the delay to the operation. It was annoying too that I had to spend the two hours between visiting times sitting around the hospital, but not with Eileen. It was not easy for Eileen either, being in a bay full of men who liked to watch sports programmes with loud commentaries. I was glad that Andrew called me from Korea, and again thanked God for my mobile.

During this Holy Week there were special early morning prayer times in the parish. I managed to get to the Thursday and Friday sessions, but I was too busy with Eileen's needs on the other occasions. There was no need to feel any guilt about this.

The operation took place on Good Friday. When I arrived to see her, she was still away at the theatre, as she had gone down later than expected. I was able to get a cup of tea and visit the little chapel for prayer. I was reading just outside the ward when they brought her back. She was in surprisingly good spirits: when they had taken her down to the theatre, every jolt had brought pain, but on the return journey there was no pain at all. I was glad to be able to leave her on a 'high' as I went to do the shopping at Sainsbury's and to pick up Chris from the airport.

When Chris and I got to the hospital the next day, we found that Eileen had been moved to her own room. Although she was prone to sickness from time to time, she was otherwise in good form. She had been sitting up for a while, and had even been encouraged to stand. We had wide ranging conversation together and more extracts from the journal.

*

My mother came on a visit to Taiwan in March. Her main object was to see her new grandson. Although her sisters had tried to dissuade her from making such a long journey, she would have none of it. As soon as she came through 'Arrivals' she had her arms stretched out to receive little Andrew. We visited several places with her in the Taipei area, including the Gladys Aylward orphanage, before taking her down south to our home in Tainan. We had wondered whether she would have enough stamina to do the trips we were arranging for her, but we need not have worried. She was indefatigable. We took her on a cross island trip, during which a falling rock bounced off the coach, but she took it all in her stride. All too soon the four weeks were up, and she was boarding a plane for home. It was the most exotic thing she had done in an otherwise quiet life.

*

Chris's visit was not a long one. He worshipped with me at the Easter morning service at St. Patrick's; then, after beef casserole and apple pie, we went back to the hospital to find Eileen in good form again. Lots more talking, and more reading from the journal. We were surprised to find her so lively after chemotherapy and an operation. The big hurdle would be the recovery of her mobility. I took Chris back to the airport the next morning. When I visited Eileen after that, we were both very sleepy, and she urged me not to come back in the evening.

75

It was as if Eileen perked up for family visitors; for the next day, when all the excitement was over, we spent a lot of time simply holding hands. Her blood count was low again and she would need two transfusions.

From this time onwards, I began to write a daily blog on Facebook. My purpose was not to complain about my current circumstances but to show that, even in adversity, there was much of God's world to be enjoyed if we kept our eyes and ears open.

*

FACEBOOK: 15 April. I find that God does not always take away the problems, but he gives us strength to face them.

*

On Wednesday morning, Eileen phoned to say that she might be moved back to City Hospital, for the staff at the Royal were not qualified to deal with cancer, and there were currently a lot of telephones calls made between the two about methods of treatment. When I reached her, I found she was in low spirits, for she had been bilious and had been unable to take much food. However, she consumed the chocolate biscuits, the broth and the grapes which I brought. During the afternoon part of my visit, she was receiving more blood. When the doctor came, he said she would remain at the Royal after all, and would go home around weekend. I hoped that Eileen would get more physiotherapy to prepare her for home living.

*

Facebook: 16 April. It seems strange not to be involved in lots of activity; but it is still a privilege to be there for Eileen in her time of need.

*

Some friends, Jenny and Peter, both doctors from Wolverhampton, were holidaying in Ireland. We had arranged for them to visit our house, but they came instead to the hospital. I arrived just as they were walking past the entrance to the ward, which was not very obvious, and was able to redirect them. Eileen was pleasantly surprised to see them, and we got caught up with

76

news of a place where we had once lived. Before they left, I gave them careful instructions as to how to cross the city. When they had gone, Eileen told me she was off the catheter now, but some adjustment was still needed before she could resume a more normal life. I was glad she was no longer nauseous, but it pained me to see her walking with a zimmer frame.

*

FACEBOOK: April 17. I like travel. But, as a full-time carer at present, there are big restrictions! However, I find other ways to travel – through family research, old journals, creative writing, use of the media and a wide ranging prayer interest.

*

The next day I arrived just as Eileen was being wheeled out to get a bone scan. Taking the whole bed meant that there would be a minimum of discomfort. It was a long process, but I appreciated their thoroughness. She was now mobile enough to go home, but would be kept on the ward over the weekend while other problems were dealt with.

As the next day was Saturday, when nobody was involving Eileen in special procedures, we were able to spend a lot of time together. Once again we enjoyed reading from the journal about our Taiwan days. Eileen's room was warm, as the sun shone right in.

*

I had to train as a lifeguard at the American air force base ready for a summer camp for American teenagers. I enjoyed these classes until I found myself partnered with a 17-year-old in an exercise to recover people from the bottom of the pool. He took his role as victim very seriously, and tried to hold me down when I sought to lift him. However, I survived.

*

FACEBOOK: 19 April. I am thinking about a small, neatly kept memorial garden just round the corner from the hospital. Just like any other war memorial, apart from one thing – the people commemorated here are all IRA members killed during the troubles.

77

When I preached at Greyabbey on Sunday I was able to tell the people honestly about my own vulnerability. We played Scrabble at the hospital and I won by a large margin. I would gladly have seen Eileen win. She had been feeling 'down'. When she said, "I do not think I have long to live", it went through me like a knife.

*

FACEBOOK: 20 April. This month I have had 2 early morning sea-bathes. I must have almost set a record for the speed with which I came out. Is there a history of insanity in my family?

*

The results of Eileen's bone scan had been positive; but they wanted to X-ray the other leg to see if it was in need of attention. She had appreciated the kindness of two nurses who were on night duty.

Sometimes we would run out of conversation, as there was not much happening. She was getting a daily injection to guard against the possibility of clotting.

*

At times in Taiwan we had special visitors. Olive Hitchcock, the then Asia Secretary of CMS, came to see us. It was not a long visit, but it encouraged us to think that someone from the mission should make a special journey in order to be with us. We were able to show her our home and the hostel and to take her to my department at the university. After seeing her off in Taipei, I went to some meetings at which John Stott was expounding the Word. How glad I was that he had included Taiwan in his itinerary.

*

Eileen had another X-ray on Tuesday afternoon. A personable young doctor called Adam, who would have been quite at home in a medical 'soap', called round and said to us: "The X-ray may reveal whether there are any secondaries in the bones of the other leg; but it is not proposed to do any further operations. We will continue to give you antibiotics for five days." So it did not appear as if Eileen would get go home till the next weekend. Our friends Peris and Teri came to pray with her.

*

FACEBOOK: 22 April. Yesterday morning, as I went down to the sea, I saw about a dozen brent geese, floating serenely in the calm water, until my visit disturbed them. Soon they will join their fellows on a long journey. After the storms of winter, when we humans think of a holiday in mediterranean climes, they prepare to take wing for Iceland and the Canadian Arctic. They are gluttons for punishment.

*

Doctor Adam called in again while I was with Eileen the next day. The X-ray revealed that there was no problem with the other leg. The purpose of the antibiotics was to increase the white cells in the blood. A urinary problem was still under investigation. I was hoping that Eileen would be home on Monday, in five days' time. I won at Scrabble again. We did not have a lot to say to each other in the evening, but it was good to be together.

*

FACEBOOK: 23 April. Reading a John Piper book, I like the part where he describes how physical sensations can increase our joy in God. He speaks of a trip to the Grand Canyon, or rising early enough to see the sunrise, or attending a symphony concert, or reading a historical novel, or putting your hand through your wife's hair, or watching Olympic gymnastic finals'. I would go for most but not all of these.

*

Both Eileen and I were able to recall a time in our lives when God was particularly close. Although there were many such times, for Eileen the greatest experience was a prayer meeting at the Faith Mission Bible College in the days of Duncan Campbell when the power of the Lord came down. For me it was during a camp in Taiwan for American teenagers (the one I was preparing for through my lifeguard training) that I had a deep encounter with God in an empty chapel. It was almost as if I could reach out and touch him.

*

From the Journal:
> *"After the meeting I asked the group to pray for me that every part of me might be under God's control. They did so, and I felt a great release of spirit. Immediately I made my way to the prayer chapel to rejoice in God and tell him that I loved him. I had such glorious freedom to do so."*

*

There may be people for whom such mountain-top experiences are very common. For most of us, however, they are those occasional encouragements that help us to get through the more mundane things of life. The memory of them brightens up many a time when life seems dull or perplexing, like the recollection of a warm summer beach on a day of driving hail.

The next day I found that Eileen was gaining a little more independence but the urinary problem had not gone away. In today's game of Scrabble I just beat her. I supposed that one of the poignant features of post-bereavement life would be that the Scrabble box would never get opened.

*

FACEBOOK: 24 April. 8.15 at the bus station. A crowd of brightly dressed elderly folk, mainly women, appears. Some are masked, others carry masks on sticks as at a masked ball. Excitedly, they climb aboard a tour bus, which whisks them out of my life. Who were they and where were they going?

*

I suppose one reason why these elderly people left a deep impression on me was that they were in good health and they seemingly did not have to cope with serious issues. It was such a contrast to our own position at the time.

80

All credit to them: they were getting toward the end of their lives, but they were determined to enjoy their days. They had not given up on life. But, at the same time, were they concerned only for the present life? When we are young, we imagine that we are immortal, but as we get older we become more and more conscious that death will come one day. Are we preparing for this?

A friend of mine began his new ministry by telling his congregation, "I have come here not to tell you how to live but to tell you how to die". He was not being morbid. If we are not prepared for the one certainty in our life, that is a serious business.

Eileen would say sometimes, "I'm not afraid of death; but I am afraid of dying, for I don't know how it is going to happen.". Many believers would echo that.

In our time of great extremity we had the duty and a privilege of showing to others, by word and example, what it meant to face death as believers. It was something much deeper than a spoken gospel message. It was a witness from the depths of our own walk with God. In a sense, we were embracing the greatest act of witness in our whole lives.

I thought that Eileen looked much better on my next visit, and it seemed there would be no impediment to her coming home on Monday. We were reading that day in the journal about Andrew's excitement at being able to walk for the first time.

The day after that, I could see that Eileen was getting bored, and was definitely ready to come home. It would mean a lot of extra work for me as her carer, but I was ready for it. We discussed my forthcoming double preaching engagement at the Chinese Church: it looked as if I would need to cancel the arrangement.

*

FACEBOOK: 26 April. The man at the bus stop chatted with a business colleague on his mobile phone for about 10 minutes in a voice that we could all hear clearly. At the end of the conversation, he said: "This is just between the two of us". Some hope!

*

I shared the story with Eileen. We needed a good sense of humour to help preserve our sanity.

It felt strange to attend my own church on Sunday morning and to hear of various activities in which, because of my circumstances, I could not get involved.

At last Eileen won a game of Scrabble. Her recent defeats were probably a reflection of her physical condition, for we would normally be well matched.

As expected, Eileen was due for discharge on Monday. I arrived, after an early lunch, to discover that we would have to wait for a letter and some medication. We had no Scrabble and no reading matter. We talked or sat in silence, played 'I Spy', and made up funny poems. At last, after 3 hours and 20 minutes, the goods arrived, and we were able to leave. Because of the long delay, we found ourselves travelling home in the rush hour.

12
TEMPERATURES AT BEDTIME

On the day after Eileen's return, we were content to relax. One way we did so was to watch an old film set during the Boxer Uprising in China. The leading Chinese characters were played by Westerners, which destroyed any hint of authenticity. I telephoned a friend at the Chinese Church to cancel my engagement, as it was not wise to leave Eileen alone for several hours.

Wednesday was the day for Eileen's CT scan at the City Hospital as a follow-up to her chemotherapy. Afterwards the registrar said that she wanted to see us. We were apprehensive, for this would normally herald bad news. "You have clots in both legs," Eileen was told. "The danger is that these could travel to the lungs. This means that the strength of your daily injection must be increased." Happily, it was decided not to admit her to hospital again. If they had done so, it would have been hard for us both to handle this emotionally.

While the cleaner was in the house on Thursday, I made a trip to Newtownards to enquire about new blinds for the kitchen. Responsibilities which would formerly have been Eileen's province now fell to me. I also bought an expensive fruit loaf in the hope that Eileen would enjoy it. I tried whenever possible to give her treats to show how much I loved and valued her; but I also knew that my very presence beside her was enough to assure her of that.

*

One regular problem that we had in our Taiwan home was the presence of rats. One day we even found one on Andrew's cradle. We put down some poison and hoped for the best. As a result, we found a dead rat under the sink unit and another under the stove. We were pleased that the poison was taking effect, but were disturbed to find droppings still in Andrew's room. We had to share our home with the cockroaches as well. No matter how well we cleaned the home, these unwelcome visitors would still come out to play at night.

*

FACEBOOK: 1 May. On Donaghadee Road there are tubs of flowers to make the area more attractive. A few days ago a little old lady was to be seen cutting the tulips and placing them in her basket to take home. Who says that vandals are all young people?

*

JoJoy came on another of her visits. She regarded Eileen as a sort of substitute mother. The two of them often shared at a deep level. That was why, despite her busy schedule as a consultant psychologist, she would still make time to fly over to Ireland to be with Eileen.

*

FACEBOOK: 2 May. When I was out jogging this morning, I saw a parked car by the lagoon with the driver's side window smashed to smithereens. Down on the grass below was an empty gas cylinder. Nasty! Give me little old ladies with a penchant for tulips any day!

*

That afternoon the three of us went to the garden centre, just beyond Donaghadee, so that Eileen could choose some plants for the yard. We had no proper garden, but Eileen used tubs and troughs to create a colourful display. It was a pity that not more people could see it. We pushed her in her wheelchair so that she could make her own choice of plants. Unexpectedly, we met Elsie, who was soon to start her chemotherapy, in the company of her sister Rhona. Eileen was glad she had made the trip, even though she felt tired afterwards. It was again a bit of ordinary life in the midst of our illness-dominated existence.

*

FACEBOOK: 3 May. Looking out of the window in the early morning, I saw a lone heron on the shore. It is always a <u>lone</u> heron. Like some people, they like to 'keep themselves to themselves'. I sometimes wonder how they manage to reproduce.

*

We had a number of friends like JoJoy who had remained single all their lives. Some of them desired husbands, but marriage never took place. Accordingly they were able to build their lives round the single state and accumulate friendships that would carry them through life. I recall at the age of 34 feeling very much alone. One day I read through Philippians 4. I claimed the promise that I could be content with the state in which God had put me, and I wept at this. A few days later I met Eileen. After spending so many years together, I now found myself thinking that, if I should lose Eileen after all these years together, I would find myself without that network of friends for holidays and social occasions which the single have built up. Would I be able to cope? I recalled the words: "Better to have loved and lost than never to have loved at all".

While I was out at Greyabbey and Kircubbin, preaching on 1 John 3:19-20 (an excellent text for helping us when we are tempted to condemn ourselves), JoJoy was preparing lunch for the three of us. Afterwards, while I was washing up and cutting up the chicken, JoJoy was putting Eileen's new plants into the tubs and troughs. It was a job which Eileen loved to do, but which she was no longer able to do herself.

Next morning I set out for the airport with JoJoy much earlier than necessary just in case the Bank Holiday or the Belfast Marathon should delay us. I need not have worried.

On Tuesday it was time to go back to the City Hospital, this time for an endoscopy. The examination was brief but uncomfortable, as she was to undergo this without sedation. When Dr. Johnston came to see us afterwards, he said there was just a bit of inflammation. Did this mean that the cancer had all gone?

One new ritual was that of taking Eileen's temperature at bedtime, just in case there should be any abnormality. Our former bedtime ritual had been to enjoy a good hug. It was only in the last eight years of our marriage that this had become a ritual, and we wondered how we had survived all those years without it. This was a tangible way of showing our deep love for one another.

We also showed that love, of course, in our regular enjoyment of sex. This was a wonderful way that God had given us to show our oneness. Sometimes, after a good time of sex, our prayers were all the better, for the capacity for both had come from God. From the time that Eileen became ill, we were no longer able to express our love in such physical ways. We were able to do so in many other ways, of course, but we missed that special act of union.

On Saturday, as Eileen was not feeling well, I got her to bed earlier than usual. When I took her temperature, however, I found that it was 38.77 degrees. We phoned the helpline and they said they would call us back. Eventually they did so, only to instruct us to go to the A&E department at the Ulster Hospital. I had to get her up again and into the car. By this time she was feeling much better; had this not been so she would have been unable to make such a journey. On arrival, she was given a blood test, and a little later saw a young female doctor called Smith. She said everything had tested as normal. We returned home and got to bed some time after 1.30. It did not appear to have been a very useful exercise.

*

FACEBOOK: 10 May. As I was reading an article on the severe Australian drought yesterday, rain was beating on the window panes. A pity we can't share our weather out so that everyone gets a good portion. Rather like we ought to be able to share our food out. But, then, we are not very good at that either.

*

The next morning Eileen seemed well enough to allow me to go to church. Afterwards, however, she felt sick and could not eat her lunch. I took her temperature again and it was 39. When I phoned the helpline they said there would be a bed for her at the City. I called the emergency doctor, as only he could authorize an ambulance, but he did not get back to us for two hours. By that time, Eileen was well enough to travel by car after all. The staff wondered why it had taken us so long to get there.

This was to be Eileen's fourth stay in hospital. We waited in the visitors' room until a place was prepared for her in a four-bedder. The woman opposite, who was from Coleraine, was being lovingly attended by her husband. When I left around 8pm, the doctor had not yet appeared to see Eileen.

13
ROLLERCOASTER RIDE

FACEBOOK : 11 May. When the sun shines and it begins to feel warm, Millisle come into its own. Yesterday was such a day. Families picnicked on the grass, and children splashed in the cold sea. I like to see people enjoying themselves.

*

At the hospital the main concern was to deal with Eileen's low blood pressure and high temperatures through appropriate treatment. She was still shivering from time to time, and it was too early to witness any significant progress. I was so glad that I did not have to observe a two hour gap, but could stay with Eileen; though there was a convention that patients should be left to get on with their meals alone. Just after I got home that evening Eileen called to say that she had responded well to her treatment.

I was reading about Peter walking on the water. Somehow I had failed to pick up the fact, in my earlier reading of this passage, that it all happened in the middle of a storm. Most of us would be very timorous about trying to walk on water in normal circumstances, but to do so in the middle of a storm would be an even greater challenge.

Storms in scripture are never simply described for their own sake. Twice the disciples find themselves in the midst of a storm on Galilee. One time the challenge is to believe that, with Jesus in the boat, they would be safe. On this occasion, seeing Jesus walk on the water in the storm represents a big challenge to Peter to do the same. When Jonah finds his ship in the midst of a storm the challenge is to be ready to admit that it is his own sin that has brought about the situation and to suggest a desperate remedy. When Paul is caught in a severe storm off Malta, the challenge is to believe God's promise that crew and passengers will remain safe and to share that information with the others. In each case, the storm represents a new challenge to faith. Now it was my own turn to face a storm, and to seek to understand how to respond to this situation by faith.

There was a minor 'storm' the next day: on the way to Bangor the car developed problems. Two bits of metal casing fell off and a sign indicated that the battery was not charging. I was still able to drive to the station, however, to catch my train to the hospital. The problem was on my mind during the visit. I had contacted a repair man, who promised to see me around 5. Eileen told me that she had definitely had an infection in the urine (probably picked up through the use of the catheter) and was about to be given more blood.

I could not stay beyond the meal break because of the car problem. My train did not get into Bangor till 5.15, which was later than expected, and I wondered if I had missed the repair man. The old anxiety was back. After a while I made another call, only to be told that he was on his way. He did not appear till 6.55. A pleasant young man, he measured the amount of juice left, and invited me to follow him to a place not far away where electrical repairs could be carried out. We put a form and some keys through the door, as the place was closed for the day, and I returned home by bus.

*

Traditionally the Chinese would regard it as their filial duty to produce two sons in quick succession in order both to ensure that the family name was continued and also to guarantee future earnings to support the family. At that time, parents in Taiwan were being encouraged to produce only two children, whilst in Mainland China it was only one.

In producing our first son within the first year of marriage, we had done exactly the right thing in Chinese eyes. Now Eileen was expecting our second child. This time she had the main part of her pregnancy in the cooler months, which was a great improvement on the first. Our second son, Christopher, was born in May 1975, just 19 months after his brother. Once again we had done everything right. At the hospital in Chang Hua, an old black-gowned Chinese granny came up to us. "Now you can have a daughter!" she exclaimed. We did not, however, feel inclined to agree with her, for we were already in our upper thirties, and had no plans to give birth to any more children.

*

Because I was waiting for the car to be fixed, I went to the hospital the next day in the morning instead of in the afternoon. This meant that I was around when Dr. McKenna and her team came round. We were told that the treatment had been successful and that much of the cancer had disappeared. In due

88

course Eileen would be able to lead a comparatively normal life. We shared this good news with Kevin when he came to visit us.

I received a telephone call to inform me that the car would need a new alternator, and that this could be fitted by the following morning. I agreed to this.

By the time I received the news, the next day, that this had been done, I was just about to arrive by train at the hospital. Eileen told me that she had just returned from having a CT scan, aimed at locating the best point for radiotherapy on the femur, to find dinner waiting for her, but it had gone cold. If I had come earlier, I would have been unable to sit with her. It really looked as if God was guiding me about the best times to visit her. A girl from Occupation Therapy called on us, and gave some good advice.

I left her in the late afternoon in order to get to the repair shop by closing time. On arrival, I was told that I needed to pay in cash; fortunately I was able to obtain cash at Asda, just across the road. It was a Cinderella-type situation, but our business was concluded just before they closed.

*

FACEBOOK: 15 May. At Bangor, three Chinese restaurant workers, laden with shopping, boarded the bus. They came to sit near me and engaged in Mandarin conversation. When I joined in I received the usual, "Oh, you speak so well"; but I sensed that they did not want to take the relationship any further.

*

After much persuasion, I went to see the doctor about my cough. It was a young woman, a temp called Dr. Gibson.. She suggested that I attend a breathing clinic and have a chest X-ray. It seemed strange to be dealing with my own problems, and not Eileen's.

I reached Eileen's bedside just five minutes before a doctor came to tell her the results of an endoscopy. More good timing! He said that there was no longer any trace of lymphatic cancer. This was great news! It really did give us some hope that there were near-normal times ahead. Maybe resurrection had merely been postponed, not cancelled. Eileen had progressed from a zimmer to a little trolley on wheels.

89

The next day we continued to feel more upbeat about the situation. We went first to the quiet room to give thanks to God for answered prayer. The plan was to follow this with afternoon tea at the coffee shop; but finding that it was closed on Saturdays, we had to go the the one in the Tower block, just beside the place where her femur had snapped. Back on the ward, Molly from Coleraine was suffering a lot of pain, and so was Angela, the young girl in the opposite corner. In the light of this, we considered ourselves fortunate.

Life during those weeks and months was still rather like a rollercoaster: it was all ups and downs. But, whereas, on a real rollercoaster, you know how the journey is going to end, in our type the destination was not so certain.

*

FACEBOOK: 17 May. I was driving home after a long day's visit with Eileen when the police turned me around at the top of Albertbridge Road. This was because a large procession was forming and blocking the main road out of town. I see no point in the 'marching season'. And it was not even July.

*

When I went to preach at Greyabbey on Sunday morning, I was able to share the good news with the congregation. I found her in good spirits when I arrived in the afternoon. Our game of Scrabble was interrupted by one of the regular visits from Winston and Betty; but it was worth persevering afterwards, as Eileen scored a narrow victory.

*

FACEBOOK: 18 May. I was glad to see my letter in 'Christianity' magazine. When we first retired we wrote an article for that magazine on the importance of 'being' rather than 'doing'. After that I got very busy! Eileen's illness has brought us back to the original scenario.

*

I went to the Ards Community Hospital for an X-ray, just to ensure there was nothing sinister behind my cough.

Eileen was still looking much brighter. Poor Angela was moved to the hospice. I brought tea and cakes up from the coffee shop, but had a spillage on the way!

Shortly after my arrival the next day, Eileen had to go down for radiotherapy. While waiting for her, I took the opportunity to look for Maud, an octogenarian friend of ours, who had an appointment with regard to her bowel cancer. I managed to find her and to escort her to the right place for waiting and also to pray with her. Eileen was moved to a different bedspace so as to be nearer the toilet. It was on that day that Molly died. I felt so sorry for her husband, who cared for her so well.

Eileen was due to come home the following day. Remembering the long delays on two earlier occasions, I was in no hurry to collect her. I turned up at 3, however, to find that she had been waiting for me for quite a while. It is impossible to get things right.

14
THE PAIN AND THE DANCE

We returned to our normal household routine. Once again my skills as a carer would be tested. Despite the recent reassurances, there was still a possibility that I would lose Eileen, and this meant for me plenty of tears.

*

FACEBOOK: 23 May. Eileen and I enjoy going through old journals. At present it is November 1975. I am working hard with my students in Taiwan and we both have our hands full bringing up two infant sons. Often I don't get to bed till after midnight. Could not keep that up these days.

*

Eileen felt well enough to cut my hair on Saturday evening. We also read in the journal about Lau Yeh's death.

*

Lau Yeh was the cook at the student hostel. The gatekeeper was called Syau Yeh. In other words, Old and Young Yeh, though the latter was no spring chicken. Old Yeh was very fond of our son Andrew, and loved to dandle him on his knee. One day I received news that he had collapsed. In Taiwan at that time you could not call an ambulance, and we had no car. At last I managed to persuade a taxi driver to drive him to the hospital. He was pronounced dead on arrival. The driver hung around, expecting to be given a sum of money to compensate him for the curse that had been laid on his car. It fell to me to arrange the funeral, for Old Yeh had come over from the Mainland with other soldiers in 1949, leaving his family behind. There was some help from an old soldiers' association, but that was all. The students, solemn-faced, gathered round the grave for the final farewell. I reflected that in future years there would be no devoted relatives to visit the grave.

*

So much of this account is about the three major issues that most of us face – birth, marriage and death. That, in brief, is what our lives are all about. The poet Philip Larkin did not claim to be a believer, yet when he saw an interesting church he would take time to explore it. In a poem that is cleverly titled 'Church Going' he expresses his conviction that the Church will continue to decline until it is extinct; and yet he feels bound to admit that only the Church can hold together these major events and give them some sort of meaning:

> "it held unspilt
> So long and equably what since is found
> Only in separation – marriage and birth,
> And death, and thoughts of these...."

Eileen felt that she wanted to go back to our local church, St. Patrick's, this Sunday. It was a major exercise to get her there, involving car, crutch, trolley and wheelchair, but we made it. Members of the congregation were warm and welcoming. To celebrate Kevin's birthday, his wife surprised him by displaying on the screen various pictures of him growing up. Eileen was determined to go to the front to receive the bread and wine rather than having it brought to her. During the hymns I felt very choked up, and it was hard to get the words out.

*

FACEBOOK: 27 May. After complaining to the doctor of a persistent cough, I found myself attending a 'breathing clinic'. I had to blow into a blue thing and the results showed up on a screen. The result was that there appeared to be nothing wrong with the lungs.

*

I had had an X-ray in connection with the same problem. When I was asked to go back for a repeat, it could have been worrying; but it was explained to me that there had been a 'nipple shadow' on the original. A second X-ray revealed that I was perfectly normal.

Our Thursday prayer meeting was moved from the church to our home so that Eileen could take part. One of our members, Peris, was about to make a prayer trip to Libya.

93

In my personal Bible study I found myself comparing two scriptures from Genesis: "Is anything too hard for the Lord?" and "Shall not the Judge of all the earth do what is right?" God is all powerful, he knows the whole picture, he is perfectly able to bring healing and wholeness, but he does not always choose to do what we might think to be desirable. There is a lot of mystery about God's dealings with us; and, if the term 'mystery' means 'revealed secret', then some of them will only be explained to us in the next life.

I had two activities on Saturday in which Eileen could not take part. One was a men's breakfast, at which the speakers were from Logos Ministries International. The other was a beach clean-up, when adults and children removed litter from the shore. We were supplied with free drinks of Coca Cola. Some of our number painted the seal sculptures that had been put in place. When the real seals arrived, they might consider these to be their greater spotted cousins from exotic climes. There was still some action for Eileen, however, for we took advantage of the good weather that afternoon for another wheelchair outing. It was good to see so many families enjoying the facilities.

On Sunday there was an 8.30 Communion service at St. Patrick's. I went to this rather than to the later combined service, so that I could be free to attend to Eileen's needs. We went out before lunch, and I wheeled her past crowded beaches. If we could enjoy such weather more often, Millisle would be as attractive as the mediterranean resorts – seaweed excluded.

The big event of the day was Pentecost Peninsula Praise, held at Greyabbey Presbyterian. At last something which we had had a vision for for so long was taking place. There was a special place for a wheelchair that fitted our needs admirably. The church was full, and there were people from at least 6 denominations. I was called upon to pronounce the benediction. In my preface to this I declared that this was the end of the beginning. We must ask God to lead us in the future so that we might understand more clearly how to give expression to our unity.

I drove Eileen to the Ards Community Hospital on the first day of the new month for an appointment about her cataracts. This had previously been postponed because of the cancer. Eileen's sight was continuing to deteriorate, and it was becoming difficult for her to read normal print. If she had had the first operation, as originally planned, she would already have been enjoying the benefit. The short operation, we were informed, would be done at the Lagan Valley Hospital in Lisburn, probably within the next six months.

When I took Eileen out in the wheelchair again, the extent of the litter,which sunseekers had neglected to take away with them, made it hard to believe we had had such a thorough clean-up.

Reading of Abraham's near-sacrifice in Genesis 22, I contemplated the place of sacrifice and obedience in my own life. At one time I was working in a very difficult parish. When the strain was becoming great, I looked up a few possible alternative jobs on the internet. When, however, I felt the Lord telling me that it was not right, I stopped. Even when people I had approached encouraged me to send in an application, I refused to do so. I was prepared to stay on in that hard parish till retirement if that was what the Lord wanted. Suddenly, when I was at peace about the decision, there was a phone call, inviting me to a new parish on the north coast of Devon. It was most unusual to be invited to start a new job within less than four years of retirement, but I felt moved to follow this up. The result was that a few months later I found myself changing jobs. On that occasion too I thought of the story of Abraham. It was as if the Lord was testing my obedience before opening a new door for me. But on this occasion, the sacrifice would not be mine to choose.

On Tuesday afternoon I took Eileen to the garden centre, where we had afternoon tea and chose flowers for our ornamental basket. It was good to be able to take Eileen to a place that was not a hospital.

*

From the Journal:
> Taiwan, 11 January 1976. *Andrew discovered a new game today. He would throw his balloon into the grounds behind; then he would shout, "Daddy, boon". It was then Daddy's job to retrieve it by climbing over the wall. Daddy did not enjoy the game.*

*

The next day we went to the Ards Community Hospital to begin a course of physiotherapy. The visits would probably be weekly, with the aim of getting her walking normally within a few weeks. A few years earlier, when Eileen broke he ankle in three places, she felt as if she would never walk properly again, but she did! This time, however, there was the additional problem of the cancer, for which allowance must be made. It was a very different scenario.

We were surprised to receive a telephone call, asking us to go to the Radiotherapy Department at the City Hospital. As Eileen had completed her radiotherapy as an in-patient, we could not understand why she should be called back. Was there to be another course? When we were called in to see a young lady doctor, we found that there had been a mistake. They had not understood that Eileen had already received her treatment. However, we were able to use this opportunity to ask a few questions and to consult a palliative care nurse about changes in medication.

*

FACEBOOK: 6 June. Yesterday I conducted the funeral of a 59 year old woman called Helen. About 40 years ago she attended a wedding where, as a teenage bridesmaid, she met the teenage best man. As a result, shortly afterwards, they arranged their own wedding, and it has lasted until now.

*

It was strange, looking back, to recall how I had hesitated to enter into marriage in case I would not be able to being enough love into the relationship to make it work. I need not have feared. Throughout our marriage, that love grew and blossomed, and here, in these months of illness, it was at its height. Day after day we expressed the intensity of our love for one another. God had been so gracious to us.

After the Greyabbey service, I was given not one, but two bunches of flowers to take back to Eileen. It was good to have the assurance of the love and care of others.

In Monday morning the chairman of our Community Association, Roy Kane, and I walked with David Birch from the Ards Borough Council round the village so that we could show him the jobs we thought needed to be done before the judges in the Pride of Place competition came round on the 30th. We would be fortunate if even half the jobs were done, but it was worth a try.

On our second visit for physiotherapy we did not need to use the wheelchair.

*

I have been power hosing the back yard. It is not a job I particularly enjoy. The main effect seems to be to transfer much of the dirt that lurked in the crevices on to my own person.

*

On my second day of power hosing, I was a little kinder to myself. The walls certainly looked better. After this, I swept up the dirt.

After completing the week's shopping, and taking my bicycle in for repair, I took Eileen for a drive via Ballyboley and Ballywalter. The road we followed was one with which neither of us was familiar. I hoped that there would be other such outings, so that Eileen need not spend too much time within the four walls of our own house.

At our prayer meeting, Peris reported back to us on her prayer time in Libya.

One task I had set myself was to reduce the journal accounts of my early days to shorter manuscripts so as to give future generations an opportunity to see what life was like in my own day without having to wade through too much material. The assumption was that there would be grandchildren to whom these could be handed down; but, at this stage, we had no grandchildren. I was writing at this stage about my first curacy in Blackburn.

*

FACEBOOK: 13 June. From the Journal, Blackburn, 2 March 1965. *The first patient I saw at the Infirmary was a boy who had swallowed a mouth organ. It was quite a joke on his ward: he was urged to stick to the piano.*

*

Eileen went with me by car to pick up my bicycle at Halford's. It was now in good shape. We both bought bicycles when we lived in Devon and enjoyed pleasant rides together on the Tarka Trail, a former railway line. In the Millisle area, however, there were no safe places to ride, and we were looking to pass on Eileen's bicycle to someone who could make good use of it. When, on our return journey, we visited the garden centre again for afternoon tea, Eileen was able to walk between the car and the coffee shop. This felt like a great achievement.

I took Eileen again to St. Patrick's on Sunday morning. As Kevin was away in France as chaplain to the forces, Gregor conducted the service. That afternoon we listened to another of John Piper's lectures, this time on John Calvin. There was much to learn from the lives of people whom God had used.

I continued to take Eileen's temperature every evening at bedtime. If it was as high as 38 degrees, we would get it down with the help of cold facecloths.

On Monday Eileen had another appointment at the Fracture Clinic in the Royal. After a long wait in the X-ray department, we were seen as soon as we got back to the clinic. Eileen received a good report and was told there would be another such consultation in six weeks' time.

On Tuesday morning we went to the Ards Community Hospital again for more physiotherapy. In the afternoon, Helen, the palliative care nurse, came to see us. When Eileen told her of her tiredness and nausea, Helen said that these things were quite normal. She also suggested some changes in medication . I had become a regular customer at our local pharmacy.

On Thursday afternoon I took down from our loft the cushions, blankets, artificial flowers and other good which Eileen had used for the relaxation classes and took them to the pharmacy, where they could be stored for future use. It was a reminder of the good work which Eileen had done among local women. It was sad to see them go, but it freed up more space in the loft.

*

In January 1976 we came home on furlough again, this time bringing our two sons with us. We spent a short time in the heat of Bangkok on the way. On arrival, we spent a few days at a CMS centre in Chislehurst called Foxbury, which had formerly been a training school for lady missionaries. Because of the time change, our sons woke up much too early. A fellow guest, instead of complaining, brought us a cup of tea at some unearthly hour. I also took the opportunity of going to Mildmay for a vasectomy. There was no way in which the Chinese granny's advice would be followed.

*

98

FACEBOOK: 18 June. One bird frequently found here is the pied wagtail. As the name suggests, it is black and white and its tail; keeps bobbing up and down. What I like most is its movement along the ground: its legs go so fast that it looks as if it is riding a skateboard.

*

I visited our chairman, Roy Kane, to talk about the garden project. He invited me to pray for his wife Marlene, who had a suspected cancer, and was due to see the oncologist on Monday. I felt sorry for them, for I did not want them to have to go through all that we were going through.

The next afternoon I took Eileen to Ballywalter, some five miles down the road. I parked by the harbour, to enable Eileen to take a short walk. We hoped to do this sort of thing regularly.

*

At an early stage of our furlough, Eileen and I went to Rostrevor for an overnight stay. This enabled us to attend the Monday night prayer meeting. It was always a thrilling experience, for you never knew what the Lord was going to do next. It was a place of reconciliation where, at the height of the troubles, Protestants and Roman Catholics could meet together to share their love of the Lord.

*

FACEBOOK: 20 June. I bought a new kind of bird food and put it out at 4.30pm, wondering whether the birds would even notice it that day. By nightfall an army of sparrows, with a little help from the starlings, had virtually scoffed the lot. It must have been gourmet stuff.

*

Eileen continued to practise her walking. On Saturday I took her to a car park near Strangford Lough for this purpose, and on Sunday we drove to the Commons at Donaghadee, to walk by the sea and the rocks.

*

FACEBOOK: 22 June. When Eileen was very ill, it was hard for her to take in spiritual truths, and she had to rely on my spiritual input. Now, however, we are able to share together from the Word of God as we used to. This is a real sign of improvement.

*

The rollercoaster was in operation again. Despite the big setback, which had given us such a gloomy view of future prospects, there were now signs of hope. Although a full recovery was unlikely, it now looked as if a semi-normal life was going to be possible, even if we did not know how long this would last.

Eileen had another session with the physiotherapist on Monday morning, and the same afternoon two palliative care nurses, Helen and Carol, came to see if the medication was working properly. We appreciated the care of so many professionals.

The best argument against euthenasia is the effectiveness of palliative care. Whenever Eileen felt that pain was coming on, she was able to receive medication that would bring welcome relief. It was not so for her aunt and her cousin, who because of arthritis, had to live in continuous pain. It is hard to understand why God allows such things. I still remember the aunt, sitting upright in her wheelchair, her face made up and her clothes neat and tidy, as if to indicate that she was not going to let the disease get the better of her. In a poem which Eileen wrote for her in 1979 she imagined God speaking to this aunt:

> "My child, I know your pain.
> Your suffering wounds me.
> My Son hung on a tree
> And I bore unbearable grief.
>
> Though you know it not,
> My arms enfold you,
> My heart yearns over you
> And I have not forsaken you.
>
> Yet a little while -
> Trust me, my child -
> And you will dance with Me

In the glory of the morning."

*

On a typical summer's day in Taiwan the temperature would rise to 37 degrees celsius and the humidity would be 90%. In such conditions we would sweat profusely even though we were not moving. We had looked forward to our time in the UK as a respite from such heat. The summer of 1976, however, turned out to be one of the hottest on record. Day after day the warm sun beat down on us. I have pictures of the boys and myself enjoying the cooling waters of Ennerdale.

*

I was delighted that Eileen felt well enough to go to her hairdresser's in Ballynahinch. This certainly improved her appearance and it was good for morale. In view of the warm weather, Betty produced ice lollies before the usual tea and cake.

*

FACEBOOK: 24 June, One unusual feature in Northern Ireland is the number of crude, hand-written gospel texts which you will find by the roadside; but maybe it was not a very good idea to put 'Prepare to meet thy God' just before a dangerous bend!

*

The good weather continued the next day, as we went to the Commons again at Donaghadee for more walking. Several other older couples sat on benches, enjoying the unaccustomed warm sunshine. But we were not without problems: at bedtime, Eileen had a high temperature again, and I had to use cold compresses and prayer.

*

Once more it was time to return with our little family to Taiwan. On 2 August I wrote in my journal:

> As the taxi pulled away from the house, I was feeling very miserable. It was my mother's remark to Christopher, 'Going tats', as if he were just going for a short outing that made me aware of the poignancy of

the situation. My mother was losing the baby she had grown to love: he would return as a little boy.

*

As the bright, sunny weather continued, we had a further opportunity to walk on the Commons. It was one of Eileen's better days. Was this a sign of good things to come?

15

DOWN BUT NOT OUT

Our life was still a rollercoaster ride. By this time a life of peaks and troughs had become normal. On the day after our walk on the Commons, therefore, Eileen had another 'down' day. She could not eat well and did not feel like going on a trip. Maybe it was not such a good idea on this day to watch 'Casualty 1909'. To see the rigours of hospital conditions in a more primitive era was not calculated to induce a spirit of calm.

*

> FACEBOOK: 28 June. When I answered the door, I found a none-too-fit middle aged man standing there, who hesitantly asked if I would be interested in a health drink. When I said not, he did not seem surprised, and meekly moved on to the next house.

*

Eileen was not fit to attend morning service with me, and, because of her condition, neither of us went to the church barbecue. I had grown very used to not going to things. However, she was able to eat her share of the chicken dinner that I had prepared for us both.

When our son Chris phoned, he told us that he and his wife would be splitting up at the end of July. They had known this would happen since April, but had not liked to tell us because of Eileen's condition. The Lord gave us great calmness on receiving the news, but we felt much sadness for Chris's sake. I remembered how Eileen once told Lauri that, when the first child arrived, she would happily go to London to give them lots of practical help. Now Chris was bearing a double burden, for he was losing the two women in his life. In the old burial service, we used to bless God because the faithful were delivered from 'the burden of the flesh'. To me this always sounded unduly negative, and yet, living as we do in a fallen world, this is not an inaccurate picture of our condition. Life has many exciting things for us, but there are also many troubles through which we have to go, and from which our death will release us.

After receiving this news, I went for a walk to think about the situation. When I saw children bathing in the lagoon, I recognized the need to bathe in God's love at such a time as this.

During the afternoon, Eileen's health deteriorated. She went to bed even earlier than usual. Her temperature was 38.41. I sponged her body and put a compress on her brow, which reduced the temperature to 37.71. Mission accomplished once more through work and prayer.

The next morning I found myself weeping again. My world seemed to be collapsing around me. I read afterwards of God's promise to Jacob and claimed it for myself. It was also on this day that the car had its pre-MOT servicing. I received a bill for £579, but through God's provision, I could afford it, and I had no worries on that score.

The day after this, members of our Community Association committee met with three judges who were vetting groups entered for the all Ireland Pride of Place awards. Our local council must have had a lot of faith in us, for ours was the only group entered by them for this award. We did our best to give them a good impression of Millisle and the improvements we had made. The sun shone, and there were even some canoeists on the lagoon. It seemed a very positive occasion.

We had to wait until November to learn the results. At a big Oscar style ceremony that included dinner, held in the Slieve Donard Hotel, Newcastle, we discovered that we were runners up within our category. This would be very good for the morale of our local people. But, on the day of our June walkabout, this was very much in the future.

Every so often, Eileen would have to undergo an MRI scan because of a lump near her ear. This was just a precautionary measure, for there had never been any sign that it was growing. When we lived in Devon, we used to go to Plymouth for this. Since we moved to Ireland, the venue was the Ulster Hospital. Because of Eileen's condition, the current scan had been postponed twice. Now, on July 1, it took place at last. We arrived early and were called before our time. It was one of the shortest and smoothest hospital appointments we had had for a long while. It was the first time, however, we had needed to use a wheelchair on such an occasion.

Getting Eileen upstairs to bed each evening was a slow process. It now required a lot of effort for her to climb the stairs. Sometimes it looked as if she

104

would not make it, and I wondered what I would do if she got stuck. It was painful to watch this procedure, for she had always led such an active life. By contrast, I would get told off for running instead of walking up the stairs!

When Kevin came to see Eileen on Thursday morning, she told him that she wanted to book a grave in the Carrowdore cemetery. She was always so practical! For me, however, it was also a chilling prospect. I could not bear to think of this wonderful body which I loved to embrace lying cold in a grave.

*

FACEBOOK: 3 July. Yesterday we looked at the pictures taken on our chaplaincy in Tunisia three and a half years ago. In the past this would have meant looking at small black and white photographs in an album. Now in this digital age it was a matter of looking at large and colourful images flashed up on our television screen.

*

We also began to look through our old photograph albums, starting with our early days together in Taiwan. As there were well over 30 of them, we were able to enjoy many days of nostalgia. It was a good way of reflecting on the many happy things which God had brought into our lives.

During my time as a carer, God gave me a lot of patience. It was a very necessary quality in the circumstances. At times, however, it was tested, as on the day when I had to make two visits to the Donaghadee surgery because a specimen which Eileen had produced was not thought suitable. On that day I lost my cool, and it showed. I am so glad that this was a rare occurrence: it would add to the frustration of the sick person if the carer showed a lot of irritation at events beyond their control.

*

From the Journal: 27 September, 1976.
> *Andrew woke up crying this morning. When at last he was able to talk, he said that his throat was broken. Eileen took him to the doctor, who diagnosed tonsilitis and an ear infection. With two sick children, it was not easy for Eileen to get any work done.*

*

105

One visitor at this time was Sue Smith, a friend from our Torquay days. I picked her up from the airport and took her to Sainsbury's to buy a few things that fitted in with her diabetic needs. When we reached Millisle I took her for a walk to show her the improvements that had been made.

Sue cooked lunch for us the following day, thus giving me a rest from my usual job. Eileen was very tired. While she rested that afternoon, I took Sue to see the new wildlife garden. Although its creation was partly inspired by Eileen's vision, she had never seen it. Because of her tiredness , Eileen went to bed even earlier than usual. This trend was worrying, for she ought to have been regaining strength all the time as a result of her treatment.

*

FACEBOOK: 5 July. Around this time of the year the seals reappear at Millisle. Yesterday I saw them on the rocks some 200 yards out from the shore. Through the scope, what appeared to be large boulders turned out to be seals, and I could even see their whiskers. And all this without leaving our living room!

*

At Greyabbey I preached on the sufficiency of God's grace at difficult times. This passage from 2 Corinthians 12 had never been as relevant to me as it was at this time. I could not have got through this period without it. God is so good to us even though we don't deserve it. I think that Yancey's book, "What's So Amazing About Grace?" should be required reading on a regular basis.

I got home to find that Sue had prepared a fine roast lunch. Eileen was in good form today, eating well, reading and taking an intelligent interest in the world around her. We watched the epic men's final from Wimbledon.

There was a meeting the next morning with a girl whose task was to advise community groups about applying for grants for improvements. I had to leave early in order to take Sue back to the airport. I returned to prepare lunch; but, because of nausea, Eileen could not eat very much.

That afternoon we went to Lagan Valley Hospital in Lisburn. The purpose was to give Eileen eye tests in preparation for two successive cataract operations. We had already postponed this twice because of the cancer. We were informed that the operation would be on August 7, but, as this was Eileen's birthday and there would be family visits, we asked for a short delay. I could not help wondering whether the operation would take place at all. After this long outing, Eileen felt tired.

Carol made another visit the next day to discuss Eileen's medication. We appreciated all the efforts that went into palliative care. The day after that we went to Newtownards for more physiotherapy. Eileen was encouraged to abandon the trolley and use crutches instead.

*

FACEBOOK: 9 July. Often our little patio is a hive of activity. In just a few minutes yesterday I saw sparrows trying to discover whether, despite the greed of the previous day, there was still some food left in the feeder, a collared dove searching the ground for any crumbs that might have dropped and starlings trying to take over the show.

*

On my way back from Tesco's on Thursday, I called at the garden centre to buy a few more flowers to brighten up Eileen's yard display. It was the first time *I* had chosen the flowers.

On Friday Eileen had one of her tired days. I hoped that, because of her treatment, such days would become rare.

*

FACEBOOK: 11 July. I have just got back from the MOT centre in Newtownards, where our 7 year old Honda Civic had its annual test. I find I get worried about arriving in time, and when asked to operate various functions, I get muddled because it is not in the context of driving, when I do things automatically.

*

FACEBOOK: 12 July. Just as I was about to sleep last night, a firework display began outside. This was one of the many celebration around the province to mark 'The Twelfth'- that time of year when

107

King Billy's victory at the Battle of the Boyne over 300 years ago is remembered.

*

At the end of the service at Millisle, Kevin said that he had an announcement to make. He told us that had been appointed rector of Movilla Abbey, and would be leaving us at the end of September. There was a shocked silence. It had been a well kept secret. His ministry had been much appreciated and he would be sorely missed.

Eileen and I had a game of Upwords, our alternative to Scrabble. And she narrowly won with 427 to my 421. I think those must be the highest scores we had ever attained. It was a good way to finish.

*

FACEBOOK: 13 July. When I was swimming in the sea this morning, a seal appeared about 15 yards away. I watched him bobbing and diving, and could even hear the splash of the water. It was a special moment. It is good to feel a part of the natural world.

*

I was quite happy to stay at home on Monday, well away from the marches that were taking place around the province. As an Englishman, I had not learned to appreciate these sectarian activities.

*

From the Journal, 1 December, 1976.
> *Christopher has a habit of taking things and putting them in unexpected places. Thus the lemon squeezer found its way into the shopping bag, the tea strainer into the bottle cupboard and the soap on to the bookshelves. We hope this phase will not last too long.*

*

On Tuesday we had an early start, as Eileen had an appointment with Dr. McKenna at the City Hospital. Since many businesses were closed for the holiday, we got there early. We were seen before the appointed time. The

108

doctor was concerned about Eileen's condition, for she should have gained more physical strength by this time. There was no ready explanation for the nausea. A lump in the groin was also worrying. She said she would arrange for another CT scan. We could not help being worried about what this might reveal. It was with heavy hearts that we drove back home.

I had to visit a woman in Carrowdore whose husband had just died. They had a large family, and the house was full of relatives. I reflected that, if either of us died, there would be hardly any family around us. There were some doubts as to whether it would be Kevin or myself who would take the service.

At our committee meeting we again talked about the garden. It was somewhat discursive, which annoyed me, as I wanted to get back to Eileen. If she had been well, she would have taken a keen interest in this.

We had a visit from a Canadian missionary couple, who were going to stay for a while at Winston and Betty's second home. The sun was shining to welcome them, but the weather later returned to its normal disappointing character.

On Thursday the palliative care nurse came to see Eileen just as I was preparing lunch. By the time I was able to serve it up, it was past its best.

On Saturday, our Community Association's dog event took place. There were 45 dogs and over 50 humans, making it the best attended such event in the peninsula. It took the form of a number of competitions, with rosettes freely awarded to winners. We used our back yard as a tuckshop. Eileen missed all the fun, as she was resting in bed.

As it happened, Kevin and I took the funeral together. Kevin had a good relationship with these people, and he was able to laugh and joke with them, sensing their mood. The service took place in the house, which meant that the majority of those who had gathered were not able to take part in it. While we were comfortable indoors, they had to suffer a sudden shower. There was no question of the widow feeling lonely afterwards with the support of such a large family. At the burial service afterwards, I was thinking that Eileen and I were likely to be buried in the same churchyard. It was a sobering thought.

On Sunday afternoon, following a good chat with our son Chris on the telephone, we listened to a tape from St. Andrew's, Chorleywood, a church much loved by Eileen; but I was sleepy, and could not concentrate very well.

109

On Wednesday morning I had a real 'downer'. I was thinking of Eileen's pitiful condition and of Chris's failed marriage, and I was concerned about whether Andrew's relationship with his Korean wife would work out well. I asked God to give me some encouragement. Did I get any? There was an offer from the Bishop to come and see us in a few days' time, and Carol promised to give Eileen a daily injection to help with the problem of the nausea.

We went to the podiatry department at the Ards Community Hospital as Eileen needed the help of a chiropodist. Things which she used to do for herself now had to be done by another.

*

It was not easy for Eileen, having formerly been a missionary in her own right, to be known now chiefly as a wife and mother. She was glad, therefore, in February 1977, to be able to organize a women's retreat. It went very well, and this gave her a spiritual uplift; but afterwards there were some trying domestic problems, which we might regard as the devil's backlash.

*

FACEBOOK: 23 July. Yesterday, when we were at Ards Hospital, someone put a tract on our windscreen that read: "Where are you going? Are you going to heaven?" We Christians are strange folk: we really feel glad to know that we are going to heaven, but we don't want to go there just yet.

*

Dr. McKenna 'phoned to tell us that the blood test had revealed kidney problems. She wanted Eileen to come to the hospital the next day for an ultrasound scan, and it was possible she would be kept in. I was glad that something was to be done, for Eileen's energy was diminishing all the time and I was at my wits' end.

On that same day we went again to the Ards Hospital for physiotherapy; but, because of Eileen's weak condition, Donna could not give her any exercises. It would have been better to have stayed at home.

110

The next morning we left the house early, prepared for the probability that Eileen would be kept in the hospital. What we did not know was that Eileen would never return to our seaside home. Maybe it was a good thing that we did not know this, as it would have been a very emotional leavetaking.

16
THREE SCORE YEARS AND TWELVE

Eileen had a blood test at the Bridgewater Suite before going for her ultrasound scan. A Dr. Khan confirmed that there was a kidney problem, and also spoke of an excess of calcium. He suggested that Eileen should be admitted as an in-patient for a week or so. It was a relief for me to know that Eileen would have special care, for it was now a struggle even for her to get out of a chair.

A long wait followed. We were given a bed in the treatment area, and there had soup and sandwiches. In the late afternoon, Eileen was taken for an X-ray, after which we went to Ward 1 in the cancer centre. I saw her nicely settled before driving home.

When I arrived at the hospital the next day, Betty had already been to see her. As she just wanted to rest, I sat there holding her hand. Later on she was able to talk more freely. The best part of the visit was when an African doctor came to see her. He said that both kidneys were affected, but that the rehydration process should help a lot.

That evening I sent more e-mails to our prayer warriors. It was comforting to know I could share our problems with so many caring friends, and I am sure that was why we were able to keep going in the midst of so many disappointments. So many times in our past, it was praying friends who had enabled us to keep going.

Preaching served as a kind of 'normal' routine in the middle of so much disruption. There was nothing normal about this Sunday morning engagement, however, for I had to find the Ardkeen church for the first time. To make matters a little more difficult, it had been moved from its original Ardkeen location to a different location near Cloughey. Although I did not know these people, God gave me an instant rapport with them.

When I visited Eileen that afternoon she told me that Bishop Harold and his wife Liz had been to see her. She was recovering her sparkle; but a little later she began to experience painful spasms in the femur of her good leg. This was ominous and extremely worrying. Once again she was taken for an X-ray. We would know the result on the following day.

FACEBOOK: 27 July. On Sunday morning I preached at Ardkeen on the love of God and with great freedom. Afterwards, over a cup of tea, a man said he thought it strange that I could call myself Evangelical and still preach on such a subject. It shows what a negative impression some people have of us.

How could I preach on the love of God at such a time as this? Surely, in our current circumstances, it must be hard to sense God's love! Or was it? He could have come like a loving parent, embraced us and made everything better; but he chose not to do so. But that did not mean that his love was absent. Although there was so much she did not understand, Eileen still enjoyed a sense of his love, that love which had been so evident on the day of Andrew's wedding. The peace which he gave her in his love was a wonderful witness both to the staff and to the other patients in the various wards where she was treated. And then what about our love for each other? It had deepened so much during this time of trial that we were almost bursting with it. Surely that could only have come from God. And where did that burning desire to exalt God before others come from? Was that not also a sign of his love? God in his love does not always do the obvious things; but that love is there for us to trace if only we have the eyes to see it.

I woke in the middle of the night and could not get back to sleep. At length I went downstairs and made myself a cup of tea. The Lord put comforting scriptures into my mind, and I drifted back to sleep at last.

My friends Declan and Peris had invited me to breakfast. I had expected something simple, but it turned out to be a cooked breakfast. I was touched by their kindness. Despite their own troubles, they had seen fit to pamper me in my own time of need.

Dr. Khan came back to see us during my visit that day. He said that the right femur was not broken, but it had been attacked by the cancer and would need radiotherapy. The kidneys were a little improved and there was less calcium in the body, but the cancer was spreading. "I know we have not yet done the CT scan," he said, "but I think we must be prepared for the prospect of death." Poor Eileen was numb, and I was grief-stricken Holding hands meant a lot to us during the rest of that visit.

My crying was getting worse. Never before in my life had I been like this. It was becoming as natural as breathing.

I reached the ward the next day to find that Eileen had had a busy time, surrounded by staff who wanted to do things for her. There were also various visits from friends. Because of all this, she did not wish to talk, and I sat quietly at her bedside. Later I took a train to our friend at Lisburn, who had offered me a meal. It was good to be able to speak to someone openly and honestly about how I felt. I got back to the ward to find that Eileen was more lively, having received more blood. We read from the journal and had a good chat.

*

From the Journal:27 March 1977:
> *This afternoon I took the boys to the university fair, where St. Michael's has a stall. Syau Chang (our new cook) was there busily preparing Spring Rolls. Eileen's baking was on display. Because of the hot weather, ice cream and cold soup were popular. I also visited the fourth year class that I taught, and bought from them some popcorn and some fish for the tank. Our children received a lot of attention – too much at times. Christopher was so sleepy that he fell asleep in the bicycle seat on the way home.*

*

FACEBOOK: 29 July. Today would have been my dad's 100th birthday. Unfortunately, he died at 68. It is not so important whether our lives are short or long but rather what we do with them. Schubert wrote 1000 pieces of music and died at the age of 31!

*

When I arrived at the hospital around 12.10, Professor Maxwell, the renal doctor, was visiting Eileen with his team. He said the stents were getting blocked. It would be necessary to replace them if Eileen was up to it, or, at least, to use a temporary procedure involving evacuation through a hole in the skin. The trouble with the kidneys was not life-threatening. Priority must be given, however, to the diseased femur, which was causing all the pain. In mid afternoon a Chinese girl, a registrar under Dr. McKenna, came to see Eileen. I

114

found her a little abrupt, and she did not tell us anything we did not already know. There were other visitors and an occupational therapist came to ask a lot of questions. I did most of the talking, as Eileen, bring heavily drugged, was in no position to respond. In all, we spent eight hours together, but Eileen was asleep most of the time and there was little meaningful encounter. At one stage I broke down and cried, and a kindly patient came over to ask if there was anything she could do for me.

*

FACEBOOK: 30 July. When you love someone very much, their pain and suffering become yours. God's love is so much greater than ours; so his suffering must be much deeper. "Surely he has borne our griefs and carried our sorrows."

*

When I arrived the next day, Eileen told me that the second femur was actually broken after all. We had visits from other renal doctors to talk about getting the kidneys to work better. There was also a visit from another oncology registrar to say that, as the cancer was still spreading, nothing more could be done about it, and she probably had just a few weeks to live. There was such a lot of information to be taken on board. It was decided to put Eileen's leg into traction until she could be moved to the Royal later in the day.

I went home in order to inform as many people as possible about the changed situation. When I was on the way back, halted at traffic lights, I got a call to say that Eileen was already being transferred. This enabled us to avoid the fiasco of her previous transfer to the Royal. I found her lying in the fracture clinic, where a nurse took some particulars. After a while she was moved to Ward 5F, where she had been before. It was like a re-run of our previous experience, except that there was now no room for optimism.

FACEBOOK: 31 July. How is it that, on a calamitous day, when Eileen was transferred back to the Royal for an operation on her second broken femur, and an oncologist said that the cancer was still spreading and the love of my life had only a few weeks to live, that I could still laugh and joke with the nurses?

*

115

I travelled to the Royal by slow bus on a rainy day. Eileen was alert, but still confused at times because of the drugs. The operation had been postponed until the morrow. I was able to read to to her from an Elizabeth Peters mystery, set in Egypt, which she had started, but would not have been able to finish by herself.

*

FACEBOOK: 1 August. At the pay desk in the hospital canteen, a notice is stuck on the wall. It begins 'SUICIDE AWARENESS'. Underneath that it says 'BEN NEVIS CLIMB'. I was glad to discover, on reading the rest, that it was about a collection and not about a demonstration.

*

I was reminded, at the beginning of this new month, that Jesus is in control of our situation. A comforting thought.

I dropped a few hints to various friends that Eileen had a birthday coming up. As Eileen would not be able to enjoy her birthday in the usual manner, I wanted to make it a very positive day in other ways. In fact, the whole emphasis from now on would be to give her the best quality of life possible within her severe limitations. A time of release did not have to be a time of negativity.

When I reached Eileen's bedside, she had not yet returned from the operating theatre; but five minutes later they wheeled her back. I was surprised at the amount of conversation we were able to enjoy at this stage; but later on she slept a lot. I was glad that she had got through the operation successfully. It saddened me to think that other patients, after a period of rehabilitation, would return to normality, whereas for Eileen there was no such prospect.

*

FACEBOOK: 2 August. I noticed that the number of Eileen's bedspace at the Royal was A1. I wish her health was just as good! Thankfully she came through the operation well yesterday and it to be hoped this will give her more comfort.

*

116

I felt that I should tell the Greyabbey folk about the deterioration in Eileen's condition; but to do so at the start of the service might cast a cloud over the whole proceedings. I decided, therefore, to tell them all at the end, and prayed for strength to be able to do so without cracking up. Strength was given. There were many expressions of sympathetic concern as I left the church.

JoJoy was due to fly in today. Her flight was badly delayed, which occasioned me a lot of waiting around. I took her straight to the hospital. Part of the time we talked with Eileen, and part of the time we read our books, as Eileen was resting. There were visits from Winston and Betty, and from their son Peter with his fiancee, Sara. Later the Bishop came: it turned out that both he and JoJoy had worked for a time at St. John's College, in Nottingham.

*

> FACEBOOK: 3 August. I have been watching a very moving film called "Inside I'm Dancing". It concerns a paraplegic lad and another with cerebral palsy. The paraplegic is a very go-ahead person, who manages to get both of them into independent accomodation, and thus changes the life of his friend, but ultimately dies.

*

David and Dorothy came to see us the next morning. Her mother had died of cancer only recently. When I brought JoJoy to the hospital, she went straight to the ward while I waited in a long queue to park the car. Why do so many hospitals have this problem? Hearing that one of the Greyabbey ladies was in hospital, I went to see her as well. It was planned to take Eileen back to the City Hospital the same day. The ambulance men came for her in the early evening, just as the Rector of the Greyabbey group of parishes arrived to see her. It was also the time when I was supposed to take JoJoy back to the airport.

On Tuesday I attended the funeral of Ian Smith, latterly in charge of CMS work in Ireland, who had died of a brain tumour. Less than a year previously we had entertained Ian and Carol to dinner in our home, unaware of the tragedy that was soon to afflict both our families. The service was a long one – some 90 minutes. I liked the idea of showing pictures of Ian's life on a screen. Afterwards I was able to chat with Carol and her siblings, all of whom I had known at St. John's Blackpool when their father was Vicar there.

117

I caught up with Eileen just as she was being transferred, in the cancer unit, from Ward 3 to her old bay in Ward 1. She told me that she was getting a lot of pain in the leg that had been repaired first. Another X-ray was called for. They were able to give her extra pain relief. Part of the time we chatted, and part of the time we were simply quiet together. In the evening, David, Dorothy and Carol, (all from our prayer group) came, and Eileen perked up to talk with them.

Our son Chris arrived the next day. Soon after the two of us reached the hospital, Dr. McKenna arrived to discuss our options. We could choose either to face further intrusive procedures in order to fight the cancer or concentrate simply on palliative care. All three of us agreed that the second was the better way forward.

"I feel you have made the right choice," Dr. McKenna said. "So many people fight on when there is not really any hope left. This is by far the wiser thing to do."

One can understand people who have no hope of an after-life fighting as much as possible to extend the life that is left. The patient is prepared to undergo any discomfort if it gives the slightest trace of hope. But somehow, when you have the whole of eternity to look forward to, this desperate action does not seem the better way.

A place would be sought at the hospice, so that Eileen could spend her final days in as much comfort as possible. We all three of us had peace about this.

After that, we spent a bitter-sweet day together. We talked a lot, but there were also times when Eileen needed to rest. Chris gave his mother her birthday present two days early – an audio book by Dawn French. This was a good choice, for it was easier for Eileen to listen than to read. After Chris returned to London, he sent various CDs of Narnia books, which Eileen would greatly enjoy during her last few weeks. When we got back to the house on this particular day, Chris, on his mother's instructions, cut my hair.

My sleep patterns remained the same. At night I would drop off to sleep easily; but often I would wake early, and if I began to think about Eileen, I could not sleep any more.

On Thursday, Chris and I took with us a photograph album from the years 1977 and 1978, and talked together of old times. The palliative care nurse,

Sandra, came to see Eileen. Eileen rejected the suggestion that she should sit out on a chair, as it would involved too much pain and discomfort.

Chris and I both took the train to Lisburn, where Jean met us and gave us a meal. On our return, we read more from the journal, and Chris found it fascinating to hear about his early childhood. When we got back that evening, we found that a lot of cards had been delivered.

*

From the Journal: 14 May 1977.

> We had a family outing after supper. The taxi took us to a place where I thought we could get Foremost ice cream, but there had been changes. We walked along Chung Shan Road to Min Tsu Road. On the way we passed several unhygienic restaurants, several clinics and finally a coffin-maker's, and wondered whether there was any connection. The children enjoyed the stalls and all the excitement of the night market. There were eels splashing in bowls and snakes in cages. We bought sunglasses for both of them, and they wanted to wear them for the rest of the trip. Between the YMCA and the cinema, we came upon a place where it <u>was</u> possible to get Foremost ice cream. When we climbed into the taxi to go home, Christopher objected. He must have wanted more excitement.

*

I was so glad that I had given Eileen such a special 70th birthday treat two years earlier. We had enjoyed a short break in Prague, which was bursting with places to visit, and the birthday itself found us eating on a cruise boat while sailing down the river and listening to the strains of a little jazz group. It was a time we would afterwards recall with much pleasure. Her birthday the following year was dominated by Andrew's wedding just two days afterwards.

Now on this birthday, which would be her last, there was no opportunity for a big celebration, involving any kind of travel. It was up to us, then, to make the most of the day, despite our restrictions. In the Lord's goodness, it turned out to be a very happy day.

When we arrived at the hospital at 12, Eileen was asleep; but after she woke she remained alert for the rest of the day. During the day she was able to read around 130 birthday cards. So often, the cards arrive only after a person's

119

death, and when it is too late to read all the personal tributes. I was so glad that I had thought to solicit cards for her birthday, while she was still alive and able to read the messages for herself.

To read the cards was to read the story of her life – her time with the Faith Mission, her missionary service, the days in Wolverhampton, our two locations in Devon, friendships in Ireland, and contacts with serving missionaries in other parts of the world and with local Chinese. Her whole life was encapsulated in one day's events.

Here are some of the things which people said:

"...you came to know the Lord at the Jack Schuler crusade all those years ago. You came into Sullivan and told us all the wonderful things that had happened to you...." (schoolfriend in Belfast)

"Seems a long time since we were young and enjoyed fellowship and fun together." (Faith Mission friend in Ballymena)

"You have left precious footprints of love and laughter in my heart." (personal friend in Aylesbury)

"...many happy memories of you radiating the Lord's presence in you." (ex-missionary in Garstang)

"...and the love of Jesus that you taught, shared and spread among us at St. James still remains today." (Wolverhampton)

"... and for the way you have touched so many lived with your caring, love and prayers for us all." (Wolverhampton)

"We do treasure all the teaching and love you gave us over the years." (Wolverhampton)

"You have been my spiritual mother, and now what you have taught me and patterned for me is carrying on." (Wolverhampton)

"You often affirmed me when I was finding things tough." (Aldridge)

"I always remember the lovely meal you cooked for us and we all enjoyed in the Church Hall when you first came." (Torquay)

"Yesterday, when I passed the Rectory, I remembered what a welcoming home you made it into." (Instow)

"We thank you for the times you shared with us during the 2008 Easter retreat in Castlewellan" (a Chinese in Belfast)

"I want to tell you that both you and Roy were inspirational to me through the Christian witness I observed during our weeks together on Alpha" (a Roman Catholic on the Ards peninsula)

"You are beautiful, and you have brought beauty and light to many." (Millisle)

"I trust you know that many people have had their lives wonderfully touched and restored by spending time with you and encountering the presence of God in the garden of your life." (Chorleywood)

"Your words of support and encouragement have blessed us richly in the years leading up to our new life in Morocco." (friends formerly in Bangor)

"I just loved the sparkle in your eyes when I saw you in mid July." (friend on furlough from Japan)

Somehow Eileen was given strength to assimilate and enjoy all these greetings and still had the energy for more photographs and extracts from the journal. In the early evening she was moved to a room of her own, and the nurses came in with a chocolate birthday cake and candles. Chris and I put up some of the cards on a notice board so that Eileen could see them. We also heard on this day that a place was now vacant at the hospice, and she could move there on Monday.

To crown it all, Chris and I went to the airport to collect the other son, Andrew, who had specially flown in from South Korea, and to bring him back to the ward for a joyful family time. It was a really happy day and a great answer to prayer. For a while we could forget the sadness of what lay ahead and rejoice in the Lord's goodness.

There were more cards to come. At the end of it all, I estimated that 152 people had written to express their appreciation of Eileen, and this while she was still alive!

Eileen was a little more subdued when we saw her the next day, but we still enjoyed being together, just the four of us. We looked at photographs, mainly of our early days in Wolverhampton and read from the journal about a family holiday in Taichung. We had a photograph taken together in which we all looked happy. In fact, I used that in my Christmas letter, and people remarked on how radiant Eileen looked. Somehow it reduced the severity of the blow.

*

From the Journal: 7 August 1977.

To celebrate Eileen's birthday we ate at King's Restaurant. We had a good meal, even if it cost a little more than it would have done at Blue Skies. Christopher fell off his chair and got a nasty bump on the head. The staff were very solicitous: one brought ointment to rub on the sore spot and another brought ice cream. He was soon back to normal.

FACEBOOK: 9 August. Now that the four of us are together for a little while, there is a sort of bitter-sweet joy in sitting together, chatting, sharing old memories and relating together probably for the last time. There is much for which we thank God, and it is good to be given this space of time when we can appreciate being together.

*

On Sunday morning, after learning in my prayers that I must trust God, even when I don't have all the answers, I set out for Ardkeen to preach on living out our Christian lives. The people eagerly took in God's Word. When I got home, I found that Andrew and Chris had prepared cottage pie; so we consumed this together with a bottle of wine.

After a delayed journey to the hospital, we found Eileen looking tireder than she had done over the past two days. Both of our sons had private time with her. Our readings from the journal were mainly about holidays. It was good to recall that time in Yuli, a little country town in the east of the island.

*

From the Journal: 16 August 1977.

For our family outing this afternoon we walked in the direction of the river. As we took a narrow track across the paddy fields, Christopher

122

*put his foot in some mud. We crossed a rickety bridge and then
studied a view that included mountains, the river and a water buffalo.
On the way back Andrew put his foot in the water. Both children,
therefore, had to have their socks removed.*

*

There were more old photographs to engage us. Some of the time we just spent
quietly holding hands. The tears welled up as I saw Eileen looking just a
shadow of her real self.

*

FACEBOOK: 10 August. So there it is. I have driven away from the hospital
for the last time after 10 months of anxious visits. Today Eileen moves to the
Marie Curie Hospice for the last stage of our earthly journey together. There is
a burden inside me that seems almost physical. But I am glad she will receive
such good care.

17
THE WORLD IN PICTURES

It was daunting to think that Eileen would spend the rest of her life in that one room. It was a pleasant enough room. There was plenty of space, it was light and airy and the window afforded a view of flowerbeds outside. There was even en suite facilities. On holiday, we would normally appreciate such facilities, but now, in Eileen's case, this was irrelevant, as she was unable to get out of bed. The bed itself was adjustable so as to give her the maximum comfort. She had all she could wish for – except the freedom to enjoy normal health in the world outside this room.

That first morning of her stay in the hospice, Andrew and Chris went with me first to the solicitor's in Bangor so that they could sign power of attorney documents, just in case at some future time I should be unable to make my own decisions.

On our arrival at the hospice, we found that the staff, both regular and voluntary, were most friendly, and we were offered tea and cakes shortly after we got there. Eileen was able to choose what food she wanted to eat, and it would arrive hot! It was a great comfort for us to know that she was being cared for so well.

For our own food, we went to takeaways down the road; then we looked at photographs from the 1983-1986 period and read of our holiday in the Pescadores, or Fisher Isles, a series of small islands between Taiwan and the mainland. There we were entertained by Mimi, who was studying in Tainan, and Eileen was able to attend a conference.

*

From the Journal: 6 September 1977.
> *For our evening meal we were taken to Mimi's house. As we entered, we found the walls were full of paintings, mainly abstract, with a preponderance of fish and of eyes. These were the work of Mimi's father. The meal was a very full one, comprising largely sea foods, which kept Mrs. Chen very busy. Both our sons were in a good mood. Christopher, on looking at a painting done by the elder of Mimi's brothers, made a noise resembling King Kong; then we saw a black tree lowering over a house and knew the reason for this.*

124

Next day, the three of us went to Marie Curie in the morning, so that Andrew could spend some time with his mother before his flight. He was very emotional as he embraced her for what could be the last time. Chris and I took him to the airport.

That afternoon two ladies came to give massage to patients who wished for it. We were a little dubious about this, as we did not know what lay behind it. Our friends Declan, Peris and Dorothy came to encourage Eileen and to pray for her. Declan was in a wheelchair because of his condition: our little praying group had really been under attack.

A photographer was taking pictures for a brochure to publicize the work of Marie Curie. He had already photographed the flower lady arranging the beautiful flowers which Andrew and Jmin had bought for Eileen's birthday. Now he wanted to photograph the owner of the flowers. As other patients were reluctant to be photographed, he was delighted when Eileen consented. He took pictures of her first with a nurse called Angela, who had already become very special to her, and then with the two of us. He also photographed the two of us browsing in the lobby. If we had known about this earlier, we might have dressed more smartly. It was all a bit surreal.

I reflected how marriage had always been a safe place for me. I prayed that God would keep me pure and wholesome in my future choices when I was left to live alone.

Chris and I had a game of tennis at Donaghadee. Eileen and I had played together in the past, but not over the past few years. He encouraged me to join the tennis club there, so that I could make extra friends after my bereavement. On this occasion I played badly: I considered that, if I joined, I might be the worst player in the club.

Eileen had plenty of clergy visits that day. Kevin had been earlier; later the Bishop came and Gill from the Greyabbey group of parishes. A social worker also dropped by. We looked at more photographs, in which our sons were growing tall, and read from the journal about our ordinary life together in Taiwan.

*

From the Journal: 19 September, 1977.

Andrew went to Kindergarten and later to Chiayi with his mother; so Christopher felt left out of things. He was glad he still had me for company; but when I was outside fixing a bolt, I heard him crying inside: he thought I had left him.

*

The door of the ensuite facility was just opposite Eileen's bed. It was there that I displayed some of Eileen's birthday cards. I also put some on the notice board, but it was hard for Eileen to see these and the flowers which were on the shelf below them, as it meant twisting her head. Each day I would remove some cards and add others so as to add variety to the display.

Each day when we returned home we longed to take Eileen back with us. This was the house which God had given her, and which she loved so much. I could not bear to think that she would never see it again.

The next day was one of comings and goings. Chris and I set off early in order to pick up JoJoy from the airport. We drove straight back to the hospice so that Chris could spend a last hour with his mother. It was a poignant moment when he gave her a hug, as it was impossible to tell whether this would be for the last time or not.

JoJoy had a long afternoon with Eileen, with no interruptions from other visitors. I wrote in my journal: *"But it is painful to see her lying there, unable to get out of bed, and waiting for the end. My heart is breaking."*

An audiobook of 'The Last Battle' was waiting for us when we got home; and these Narnia recordings, sent by Chris, would continue to arrive over the days that followed.

*

FACEBOOK: 14 August. It was good to have both sons around for a few days. It was also poignant, as the four of us may never be together again. It looks as if we shall have to establish a new dynamic for the three of us.

*

Eileen was feeling groggy on Friday morning, but, as a result of some intravenous feeding, she was feeling somewhat better for our afternoon visit. JoJoy and Eileen had some time on their own. Eileen said she would try to record messages to various people if she felt well enough to do so. It was a brave venture to tackle

*

FACEBOOK: 15 August. The Tall Ships are in Belfast. Despite the rain, a lot of people have turned out to see them. There is a grandeur about those old sailing ships. Unfortunately, I have other priorities....

*

The following day, since nurses were working in the room, and a doctor who came wanted to see her alone, and because JoJoy wanted more time alone with Eileen, I did not feel that I got any quality time with her. At the conclusion of Jojoy's visit, we had Communion together. After this, I took JoJoy to the airport. I set out early in case the visit of the Tall Ships should cause traffic delays; but I need not have worried. I saw a few of these ships from a distance as I sped along the motorway. JoJoy said she fully believed that God would heal Eileen, and urged me to send prayer warriors to pray with her about this every day; but this was not my own vision, and it left me feeling very confused.

When I returned to Eileen, she was feeling very tired and was experiencing bowel problems. In the light of this, we could not talk very much.

After my morning preaching, I was able to spend Sunday afternoon with Eileen. Apart from a visit from Betty, I had Eileen to myself. . I read to her again from the Egypt book. Eileen said that JoJoy had given her a prophetic word from Chorleywood that people should pray life, not death, into this situation.

Monday was a time for family visits. When these visitors had gone, she wanted to rest for a while. Later we looked at a photograph album and the journal, and watched the news on television. This, at least, was part of the ritual we would have followed if we had been at home together.

*

127

From the Journal: 12 November 1977.

As the orange season was upon us, we began this afternoon to cut up oranges for marmalade. We were towards the end of the job when the phone rang. It was my mother phoning from Blackpool. Dad had been haemorrhaging in the night and the doctor had given him only a few hours to live. A quick decision had to be made.

Eileen packed a bag for me, and I caught the next flight for Taipei. There, in the capital, I discovered that, because it was a holiday weekend, I was unable to get through the procedures needed in order to leave the country. My father had died by this time. My anxious wish now was to get alongside my mother as quickly as possible. During the time of waiting I hated to be alone. I therefore sat with Bishop Pong in his flat, went with a doctor on his rounds and took a Hawaian Chinese out for a meal. I had never lost anybody so close to me before, and I found myself getting very tense.

After the weekend, I was cleared to leave. I was able to board a BA flight, having borrowed money from the diocese; but the aircraft broke down in the Middle East. I recall pacing up and down a yellow corridor in Bahrain Airport, grimly mouthing the words 'Praise the Lord' because a book had told me to do this. There was great rejoicing when the 'plane was repaired; but even when we got to Heathrow there was delay because someone had got into the cargo hold in Colombo, and the luggage had to be inspected.

I got home the evening before the funeral, and was able to see my father's body. After the funeral, I stayed to look after my mother for two weeks. During that time I became very shivery and had a poor appetite, and it was in that condition that I started back for Taiwan. I found myself in a Jumbo jet full of pilgrims returning to Malaysia from Mecca. Owing to delay, we missed our ongoing flights from Bangkok, and had to be put up in a hotel. I was urged to enjoy free food, but I was still cold and had no appetite. However, when I woke on a bright and sunny morning, the symptoms were all gone. It was like a resurrection. In fact, when I think of death and resurrection, my mind often goes back to this experience.

*

In the intervening years, I had lost my mother, but on this occasion had the satisfaction of being with her in the closing stages of her life. I was surprised at how peaceful the ending was. Nevertheless, it was hard to sing the hymns at her funeral.

This would be my third major bereavement, and the one which would affect me the most deeply. Eileen would often tell me that she was ready to go. "I do not fear death", she would tell me, "but I am afraid of dying". I think many Christians would echo those words. It is like the much feared door in 'The Last Battle'. Many are afraid to go through that door, but on the other side all is joy and splendour.

My tears at that time had a twofold origin. In a sense I wept for Eileen, for all the pain and discomfort, the privation, the uncertainty that this faithful servant of the Lord was going through; but I also wept for myself, and for the pain of her loss which I was going to feel so soon. Even when we have the Christian hope to sustain us, the pain of separation is still very real.

On Tuesday I visited Eileen earlier than usual. She was going through a spiritual battle. The devil was seeking to destroy the peace which God had given her. God sent the chaplain, Marlene, to minister to her; and later on Kevin also came to help her. There were other visitors too. When at last we were alone, we just enjoyed being quiet together. I did not feel very strong, for it was as if my whole world was collapsing.

The next morning, as I prayed and read the Bible, I did not get any word from the Lord. I felt abandoned, but prayed that the devil might not win. Fortunately, this sort of thing did not happen very often. As I drove to the hospice, Vaughan Williams's 'Dives and Lazarus' was playing on Classic FM. I recalled the words of the hymn, written to that tune:
> "I came to Jesus as I was,
> Weary and worn and sad;
> I found in him my resting place
> And he has made me glad."

While I was with Eileen that afternoon, there were visits from the social worker and a lady doctor. The social worker, a Christian, asked if I had the resources to cope with bereavement, and I said that I felt that, with God's help, I had. The truth is that we cannot really answer such a question until the event happens. The doctor assured Eileen that she would not need to be moved anywhere else, that she had either days or weeks left to live, and that there would be no sudden and painful deterioration.

When I arrived on Thursday, Gregor was with Eileen. The Bishop had already been. I was grateful for all this pastoral care. We did the usual reminiscing, and she closed her eyes for part of the time. Scrabble remained in the drawer: maybe, I thought, we would never play together again.

On Friday, Eileen's bed was wheeled outside for a time so that she could feel the touch of the sun and the wind, things which the rest of us so easily took for granted. This meant a lot to her. Otherwise, we looked at photographs as usual and read from the journal, and I read more of the book set in Egypt. I also brought with me an A4 photograph I had taken that very day of the view of the yard and the sea which she enjoyed while sitting in her chair at home. This was part of my campaign to help her, during these days of confinement, to enjoy as much of the world outside as I possibly could. Gradually these photographs would replace the birthday cards.

When I arrived on Saturday, Eileen told me that Liz, the Bishop's wife, had been to see her, and brought her a very meaningful card. Their relationship went back a long way; for Liz, as a teenager, had met Eileen when she was a Faith Mission worker in the south of Ireland, and had subsequently been a prayer partner of this 'Eileen Gordon' as she embarked on her missionary career. We had a game of Scrabble after all. I gave Eileen some help, and ended up being beaten by 50 points. We tried to make these into fun days, despite the limitations.

When I preached on Ardkeen on 'spiritual warfare', the people said that it met them at a point of need. It had reference to my own needs as well.

During my visit that afternoon to Eileen, I finished reading the Egypt book to her, and we began reading a Christian book with the appropriate title, "All the Way to Heaven". On her own journey to that place, Eileen had reached a plateau. Much as it broke my heart to contemplate our separation, I was ready to release her earlier rather than later, so that she could be spared a long period of such restriction. It was a time of slow release for both of us.

I prayed the next morning that God would show me how the love which I had for Eileen could be used later to bring benefit to others. I was so glad that we could tell each other time and time again how much we loved one another.

Words barely sufficed. Though all else might be taken away, our love just grew deeper.

I visited the wildlife garden and took a photograph, so that I could show Eileen what it was like. This was to be the second picture in the new display. I also wrote to the Youth Justice Agency concerning Eileen's vision to employ young people on allotments there.

I was glad to see that Eileen had had her hair done, as this was good more morale; but it had left her feeling a little tired. We managed to play Scrabble again, and I scored a major victory.

All through this time, I was impressed by Eileen's courage and her acceptance of the situation. Seldom did I hear any word of complaint. I wondered how I would feel if I were placed in such a situation. I think it was Spurgeon who said that God gives his grace not for hypothetical situations but for real ones. It is foolish, then, to speculate about such things. The big difference for me would be that I would have no caring spouse to help me through my difficulties.

*

From the Journal, 31 January 1978.
> *Just before the children's bedtime we were talking, and I said that we must throw the kite away. Andrew misheard. "What do you want to throw the cat away for?" he asked.*

*

Dr. Regan talked with us on Tuesday. There was still a great desire on the part of the staff to satisfy any need of which Eileen might become aware. She was already receiving help in making recordings for us to listen to after her death. There did not seem to be any easy answer to the problem of her tiredness.

*

FACEBOOK: 26 August. One of the nurses at the hospice said that when she enters our room she feels a sense of peace. A real answer to prayer.

*

131

I continued to bring photographs for the display. There was one of the beach in the Algarve where Eileen had swum in October for the last time. There was one of our Korean-type Christmas meal at Jmin's family home in Seoul taken during our visit at the end of 2007. Eileen looked so happy in that shot.

On Thursday I went to the local doctor's surgery to have an ingrowing toenail removed. He froze the foot first, and I suffered no discomfort. It made a change to be getting some medical attention myself. While I was in Donaghadee, I went to Bow Bells for my lunch. I had previously seen the odd lonely pensioner sitting there: now that person was myself. It took some comprehending.

Eileen was tired that afternoon, but was happy for me to read to her. An occupational therapist suggested various ways in which she could occupy her time. Under normal conditions, this would be no problem. She would happily have exploited her talents for patchwork, painting and other skills. Now she was being invited to do things which any child could do. Another tugging at the heartstrings.

*

From the Journal: 25 March 1977. (Andrew is in hospital in Changhua and Eileen with him.)
> *When Christopher and I entered Andrew's room, his eyes did not light up with recognition. He told us that Mummy had gone to buy a 'lorry' for Christopher. On seeing me, she wept. It was a bigger ordeal for her than I had realized.*

*

We get answers from God when we pray in faith. But what did it mean to 'pray in faith' in our current situation?

When I arrived at the hospice on Saturday, Eileen was asleep, but she woke after half an hour. It was another of her sleepy days. On the daily visit with Winston, Betty was wearing dark glasses, having just had a cataract operation. Now we knew that Eileen's operation would never take place.

One routine we followed while Eileen was in the hospice was that I would park my car near the window of her room. When I left to go home, I would

132

look in through the window and we would blow a kiss to one another. On the odd occasion that she did not respond, I would drive away in tears.

*

FACEBOOK: 30 August. I took a walk along the coast on behalf of both of us. On the way I saw youngsters canoeing on the lagoon and a cormorant diving. I was able to share these things with Eileen when I went to see her.

*

I attended the combined service at Carrowdore on Sunday morning, but during the worship I felt thoroughly miserable. I think this was because I was aware that the next time I attended that church it would be for Eileen's funeral.

Eileen and I had Communion together that afternoon. This was a much better time of worship for me. I did not know whether Eileen's tiredness was a mark of her deterioration: I held her hand, and, as I looked into her face, the tears welled up once more in my eyes.

On Monday, for the third day running, Eileen was very sleepy. Was this the beginning of the end? We tried a game which the occupational therapist had brought, but Eileen could not handle it. She was happy, however, for me to read to her from the book about preparing for heaven and from a Tess Gerritson thriller.

Another month was ending. It was unlikely that Eileen would still be with us at the end of the month that was to follow.

18
A KIND OF HEALING

One day I said to Eileen, "When you have gone, I am going to cherish myself, just as you have cherished me."

Eileen smiled. "I have never heard you say that before," she exclaimed.

I had long had a tendency to put myself down. I would deny myself little treats, but I was very happy to provide treats for Eileen or for both of us. One of the joys of marriage lay in giving pleasure to my wife. With the prospect of a return to single life, I was going to have to learn how to be kind to myself. Eileen was reassured to hear me say this. It seemed that I was learning at last.

At this time I seemed to weep more and more; but I took comfort from the words of Psalm 27:
> "The Lord is my light and my salvation -
> whom shall I fear?
> The Lord is the stronghold of my life -
> of whom shall I be afraid?"

On the first day of the new month I cast my mind back 11 years. Earlier in that year, Eileen had been visiting her sister. It was a hot day, and, on the way to buy ice cream, they went to look at some houses that were being built. The builder stood in a doorway, and told them: "This house is not sold yet". Purely out of curiosity, the two sisters went in. As Eileen gazed through the window at the clear blue sea, it was as if the Lord said to her: "This is your house". She shared this with me on the telephone, and we agreed to buy it. It became fully ours at the end of August. As I was recuperating from a small operation, and this gave me some extra leave, we decided to stay in our new home for the first two weeks of September before letting it out to others. It felt strange at that time to be living in a house that was ours, yet which contained none of our history.

Now the situation was very different. We had put our stamp on it. Paintings and tapestries done by Eileen hung on the walls. Chairs upholstered by Eileen stood round the dining table. Our books and recordings were on display. More than this, the house was full of happy memories. God had been so good to us. It also served as a base for offering warm hospitality to others – a tradition that I hoped I could observe even when I was left alone.

Eileen had several visitors on this day. She slept from time to time. Still she enjoyed a God-given peace – something which the doctors found hard to understand. The next day Eileen told me that they had started giving her anti-depressants; but when she explained that she had peace already, these were withdrawn. She was also receiving more fluid, because the kidneys were dry.

As Eileen did not feel like eating her evening dessert, I usually ate it instead. One day Vicky, the woman who served us, wanting to be kind to me, produced two desserts! Later she accepted that the dessert would go to me instead of to Eileen, and she would ask me rather than Eileen to make the choice.

On Thursday morning I drove to the International Airport to pick up JoJoy again. During the long visit that followed, I spoke less to Eileen so as to give JoJoy more opportunity. In the afternoon, members of our prayer group (Declan, Peris and Dorothy) also came. They prayed for Eileen's total healing. I did not add my own prayers for this, as I had no conviction that this was going to take place, much as I longed for it to happen.

The whole experience left me feeling very confused. I wanted Eileen to be healed more than anything else in the whole world, but I did not have faith that this was going to take place. This is a dilemma which others have faced beside myself. We know that God is able to heal all kinds of diseases, and there are stories of truly miraculous recoveries. Eileen and I had sometimes held healing services in our churches, counting it a great privilege to pray for those who came to us in need. We knew that prayer for healing was to be a regular ministry of the local church rather than waiting for a person with special gifts to come along. Healing, however, is not a result of our own efforts: it comes from the Lord. Sometimes he heals, sometimes he does not. There is no easy explanation as to why this should be so.

Sometimes Jesus was hindered in his healing ministry because people did not have enough faith. Would Eileen have been healed if I had had more faith? It would have been unwise to have gone along this road, for it could have left me feeling guilty about my lack of faith. That would have been a false guilt.

Sometimes God gives us a special faith, so that we <u>know</u> he is going to heal; but I have not often had that assurance. Sometimes we pray, "If it be your will", or we even speak of the 'healing' of death? Is this just a cop-out? I think not. What it all boils down to is that we place ourselves and our loved ones in the hands of God. He knows what is best for us. We trust that we shall see his hand on the situation, however things may turn out.

A friend had also lent me a book called "You Can Be Healed". I read it, but I found the whole thing too glib. It was as if, having the right formula, you could command healing in virtually every situation. This was not my experience.

*

A renowned healer, Father Francis McNutt, was coming to Kaohsiung to conduct some meetings. We went along in order to get some prayer for Andrew's flat feet. It was a dramatic occasion. We were talking with a taxi driver, who was queuing with us. The next moment he was lying on the ground, 'slain in the Spirit'. He was one of many such. A little girl with polio began to show some improvement. Others were touched. A Chinese pastor tried to persuade me to go up and help with the ministry, but I felt I was there to receive rather than to give. This man's international healing ministry continued afterwards for many years. Yet even if he had come to visit Eileen in her terminal illness, I have no guarantee that God would have arrested the disease.

*

FACEBOOK: 4 September. I like music. The problem is what kind of music to enjoy in my present circumstances – sad music to chime in with my mood or joyful music to lift me out of it? I suppose good worshipful music is best at the moment.

*

The next morning we set out early to pick up Chris from the City Airport. While the three of us were with Eileen, several other visitors came. Our friend, Mary Edwards, had sent some photographs taken at Chris's wedding in 2002, and I added these to the growing display. Eileen had looked so radiant on that day in her colourful costume. These pictures drew forth plenty of comment. Later I took JoJoy back to the International Airport. She had sacrificed a lot of time in a busy schedule to visit someone who had been like a mother to her.

On Saturday the new wildlife garden was opened. Chris helped me to set up a gazebo, and also took some photographs for me. The opening ceremony was performed by our brilliant MP, Lady Sylvia Hermon. As she prepared to cut

136

the tape, she said publicly some kind words about Eileen. I took her for a walk round the garden, after which we ate sandwiches together with Kaye, our treasurer. Sylvia had recently lost her own husband after a long illness, so we were well able to sympathize with each other. Chris and I left before the Fun Day got under way. I took with me a picture of the opening ceremony to add to Eileen's display.

Chris and I spent most of the rest of the day with Eileen. When I went out to buy fruit juice for her, Chris was able to spend quality time with her. That evening, on his mother's instructions, Chris gave me a haircut.

While I preached at Greyabbey on Sunday morning, Chris spent extra time with his mother. A churchwarden was kind enough to drive me to the hospice after the service. Chris had to catch his return flight. There were several other visitors. When they had gone I read to Eileen from the Christian book and the thriller. Heaven was getting nearer all the time. It was my turn to get sleepy: part of the time we simply held hands in silence. When it was time to leave, I longed to scoop her into the car and take her back with me.

Over these days I continued to add to the display of photographs. There was a picture of the harbour at Bunbeg in Donegal which we had visited on a summer holiday just before Eileen became ill. There was also a picture of the two of us looking very happy at a family meal held to celebrate our combined 70th birthdays in September 2007. There were also smaller photographs, that included a beautiful garden in the New Forest, and autumn trees and classical buildings in the grounds of Princeton Seminary. God had been good to us, and had given us lots of wonderful adventures.

*

We attended the missionaries' annual conference in Taichung in July. While we were there, I had some back trouble. On the Thursday morning, when I tried to get up, I collapsed back on to the bed in pain. Instead of attending the first morning meeting, therefore, I stayed in bed. Andrew decided to stay back and take care of me. He told me he was the doctor, and proceeded to give me 'injections' and to perform an 'operation' - both painless, I am glad to report. At break time, Eileen brought two friends to pray for me. After this, I was able to get out of bed without a lot of difficulty and get to the next meeting. We have both experienced at time that God does heal.

*

On my way to the hospice, I bought a book of worship songs that included 'King of Kings, Majesty', which Eileen had requested for the funeral. She was looking more tired today, but we were still able to do the usual things. A man in another room near to her had died, and I could see the reaction on the faces of his relatives. I wondered for how long I would still be able to hold Eileen's living hand.

*

FACEBOOK: 8 September. I was reading how God is my salvation and my fortress. Amid all the uncertainties of the outside world, I have always found that my marriage has been a safe place. Now, with this option fast disappearing, I am forced to look at my real 'safe place', which is God himself.

*

A friend telephoned to say that, as all the signs pointed to Eileen being at the last stage, Andrew, newly returned to the UK, should be urged to come over immediately. This message greatly increased my grief. When I checked this out with Dr. Regan on her visit, however, she said there was no expectation of an early demise. As a result of the call, Andrew and Jmin decided to come over a few days earlier than planned. On this day, I managed to finish reading the Gerritson thriller to her.

The next morning I enjoyed reading from Romans 8, and looked forward to sharing it with Eileen. It was still our custom that I would share regularly with Eileen what the Lord had taught me from the scriptures. God's love would never leave us, even though death should intervene.

I collected Andrew and Jmin the next day from the International Airport and brought them to see Eileen. Some good, positive conversation followed. I was pleased to see how well they were handling their return to British life.

*

FACEBOOK: 10 September. Some time ago I wrote to Judi Dench's agent to ask her to send a greeting for Eileen's birthday, since Eileen admires her work. Yesterday I received a signed photograph from Judi and look forward to surprising Eileen with it today.

*

In the late morning I drove Andrew and Jmin to the hospice. Eileen was really glad of their company. There were other visitors too. We talked, among other things, about Chris's situation. *"Just before we left, Andrew burst into tears and hugged his mother for what was probably the last time. Our family dynamics are changing greatly. Nothing will be quite the same again."* I took them back to the airport and drove home in the gathering dusk. I had a painful back during the night.

I continued to add pictures to the display. There was a picture of us in Arab costume, about to ride on camels in a desert area of Tunisia. We called ourselves 'Lawrence and Florence of Arabia'. There was also a picture of some flowers taken in the mountain fortress village of Boussages in Languedoc, where we had stayed for a fortnight in the house of some friends. Another picture showed our family spending our last Christmas together in our seaside home.

I was Eileen's only visitor on Friday afternoon. She was growing more sleepy and was getting a little confused. I felt I was gradually losing her, and it hurt me greatly. But I was still able to read to her. She wanted the Lord to take her soon, and I had to be ready to release her. Today, when I blew my kiss outside the window, there was no response....

I had no back trouble the next night. Two members of the RSPB led us in a bird recognition walk that I had arranged through the Community Association. There were nine local people on the walk. On the flats left by the tide, we observed plenty of activity. In addition to the 'usual suspects', we saw a bar-tailed godwit and a rock pippet. If I had been on my own, I would not have been able to identify these.

I reached the hospice in the middle of an emergency. Eileen had been placed out in the sun, but the mattress had deflated and she was in agony. I rang for a nurse, as the buzzer was still inside the room, and she was brought back inside as soon as possible and given some medication as the bed was reflated. This left her sleepy for a while, but after that we had normal contact, which included reading things out to her. At meal time,. Vicky brought me two courses. When I left, Eileen waved back!

139

I worshipped at St. Patrick's on Sunday morning. I was not on such a 'downer' this time, as this church building would not be associated with Eileen's funeral. We had Communion together, and I read to her a lot. Although I tried to crowd as much as I could into these visits, I felt it was a boring existence for her, and it would be a mercy if the Lord were to take her. I recall her saying to me one day: "I have the easy part. All I have to do is lie here and be looked after. You're the one who has to do all the rushing about." But if I had the choice, I would choose the rushing about any time. In her attitude to her suffering, she was a shining example, and I would never forget this.

*

We planned to leave Taiwan in the spring of 1979 and find work back in England. Already, in the previous autumn, we were beginning to prepare. I posted parcels of books back, so that we would not have too much heavy luggage at the time of moving. But this created problems, as the entry for 3 September reveals:

Andrew did not like to think that his things might be sold. When I told him we could not afford to send all the things back home and send Daddy too and asked him which he preferred, he said he preferred the toys. So much for Daddy's worth!

*

When I got to the hospice on Monday, a young doctor called Chris was explaining that anti-depressants could be of value even in our situation and he left us to make our own decision. We called JoJoy for advice, and she told us that it would fulfill a biological need, and was no indication of lack of faith; so we agreed to the treatment.

In the late afternoon, Mel and Carolyn (who had seen the skylark with us on that long distant day) came to see us just before ending a short visit to Belfast. We exchanged some brief but cheerful conversation. Eileen seemed more alert today: there were no periods when she dozed off and left me to my own devices.

The next morning I found listening to some Graham Kendrick music uplifting, and I even found myself dancing to it, which was highly unusual for me. I came down to earth again, though, when I reflected that Eileen, who loved dancing, would never do so again – at least, in this life.

140

When I reached the hospice late in the morning, I found I had to wait with Winston and Betty until Eileen had been washed. How difficult it must be to have the most basic functions carried out by others. There is not much dignity left when you are seriously ill. Over the days that followed, this became more and more true. What could not be taken away, however, was her dignity of spirit.

After lunch she told a nurse that she felt sickly, and was given an injection. This must have been powerful stuff, for she was asleep for a long time afterwards. As I looked at my dearest one, who was always so alert and so able, lying there asleep, my eyes filled with tears again. She regained consciousness just before meal time, when Gill was coming on a visit.

*

> FACEBOOK: 16 September. We have lived with uncertainty for over 11 months. It is the not knowing how many days we have left that is difficult. I have always liked to plan ahead and get everything right. Now it is just a matter of living one day at a time and leaving the planning to the Lord. A hard lesson.

*

Just before I set out for the hospice on that Wednesday, Winston phoned to tell me that there had been a deterioration in Eileen's condition. This made me very apprehensive when I was on my way to see her. She was still able to recognize me, and I was still able to read to her, but communication was difficult. It was a real fight for her to stay awake. I had to keep encouraging her to drink from a cup of tea, and she only picked at her food. Chris, the GP, said he did not know whether this condition resulted from the medication or from the illness itself, neither did he know whether this was part of a continuing deterioration or a lower plateau. My heart was heavy.

*

> FACEBOOK: 17 September. I have been re-reading Sheldon Vanauken's "A Severe Mercy", in which he writes of his love for his wife, who died young. As Eileen's condition continues to deteriorate, the situation is certainly severe; but I am praying for a fresh awareness of God's love and mercy at such a time.

141

*

When I was running, I saw a heron at the water's edge in the pink glow of pre-dawn. In my Quiet Time I held to the assurance that God is good.

Eileen was no worse. We were able to do some reading together. She had a good sleep in the middle of the afternoon. A schoolfriend called Joan came to see her. The two of us talked while Eileen listened. One must always assume that the sick person can hear and understand all that is being said, even when there is little evidence of it. Both of our sons telephoned, and Eileen was able to exchange a few words with them. Where would we have been without our mobiles at this time of emergency? Chris was wondering whether to come back over earlier than planned. Andrew and Jmin were buying new things for their home.

Eileen's main problem the next day was diarrhoeia. She had been changed several times and was feeling very sore. It must be so hard to lose control of one's private functions. The nurses who came to attend her were very cheerful: this was something they had to do regularly for their patients. It was a further loss of dignity. Eileen's hands were shaking, but she stayed awake throughout my visit. We finished reading the 'heaven' book.

Elizabeth Sherrill ends her book by describing the death in hospital of a friend called Mea – a woman who had not followed the Lord during her normal life, but who seemed to change in her final moments. The last words she was heard to say were "Goodbye until the morning".

We have such a hazy idea of heaven. The way it is often presented, it sounds like a dreary place, like a boring and never-ending church service. How different the reality must be from this. It is the place where we shall see God's glory. The word 'glory' means 'heaviness'. I think C. S. Lewis was inspired when he wrote in "The Great Divorce" of heaven being a place where everything was solid as opposed to the place of shadows where we now live.

I sometimes think back to those times when God has been most real to us. For Eileen the highlight was that prayer meeting at the Faith Mission Bible College; for me it was that little chapel on the campsite in Taiwan. These deep experiences of the Lord's presence, though very meaningful at the time, were but a foretaste of the joy of heaven. If we can recall the joy we have felt on such occasions and multiply this many times, then we may have some slight

142

inkling of what heaven is like. It is to be anticipated as the fulfilment of all our earthly longings, the culmination of our love affair with God.

When you have had even a tiny glimpse of heaven, the ordinary things of life seem so unimportant. We have to decide which clothes to wear, what we shall cook for dinner, how to manage our finances and a host of other choices which pale into insignificance in the light of eternity. Seeing Eileen on the brink of her heavenly life, I wondered whether my attitude to this world would ever be the same again.

I love the words of the Unicorn towards the end of C. S. Lewis's book, "The Last Battle": "I have come home at last! This is my real country! I belong here. This is the land I have been looking for all my life, though I never knew it till now."

By this stage I was becoming more and more reluctant to leave Eileen and go home, as our time left together was so short.

*

FACEBOOK: 19 September. You never know whom you are going to meet on Facebook. My latest 'friend' is a Chinese girl who served as interpreter when I took a party of doctors, nurses and teachers to Fengdu, in Sichuan province, seven years ago.

*

I really felt low on Saturday morning. In my great grief, it was as if I had nothing left to live for. Through a psalm God assured me of his steadfast love.

On this day, Eileen was still very sleepy and a little nauseous. I read to her a little. Although our love was still there, I did not find a lot of joy in being together under these strained conditions. Eileen had assured me, "I am still the same inside", and that was something to hang on to. Because of her incontinence, she had to be changed twice while I was there. Emotionally, the whole thing was taking a heavy toll upon me.

*

FACEBOOK: 20 September. At the men's breakfast in Carrowdore yesterday, I met Michael for the first time. He comes from Ghana, spent four years in Italy, joined the Forces and served in Iraq. Now he is doing extension training to equip him to serve as a minister of the Church. Surprising whom you can meet in a remote corner of Ireland.

*

When I was preaching at Greyabbey, I was able to speak boldly about my relationship with God under my current circumstances. Those moments of despair were not the norm. Most of the time I was conscious of God's upholding, and I took delight in sharing this with others.

Afterwards I took part in a meal at Carrowdore which had been arranged as a send-off to Kevin and his family. I did not stay for the speeches, but broke off as soon as I could so as to get to the hospice. I was unprepared for what I found when I got there.

19
FIVE DAYS AND NIGHTS

When I arrived at the hospice, I found Eileen much failed. In view of this, I telephoned my sons, and Chris arranged to come over right away. Although I sat all the time with Eileen, conversation was virtually nil. All I could do was read the books and magazines I had brought with me. I met Chris off his 'plane at 9.25pm and took him straight to the hospice.

A night nurse told us, "I don't think she will last the night". Hearing this, we decided to stay through the night. I used a camp bed and Chris the long seat.

From 2 till 4 Eileen was in some distress: she vomited bile, and there was phlegm in her throat that she could not dislodge. After that she seemed more peaceful. Chris had three or four hours of sleep but I had only brief dozes. Eileen had lasted through the night after all. We were provided with breakfast. Afterwards Chris drove to the house to collect some things while I stayed with Eileen. Kevin made his last visit. A young mother came from Millisle with a little card and a music CD. Winston and Betty came on an extended visit. The Bishop, on his visit, read some prayers to prepare Eileen for death. In the middle of the day she was a little more responsive, especially while the Bishop was with us, but that did not last. For our other two meals, Chris and I were given soup and sandwiches.

As an experiment, to see whether Marie Curie could help such people, a young man with Downs Syndrome was placed in the room opposite. He watched children's programmes on his television most of the time, and seemed to be enjoying himself.

So we came to our second night. Once again it was not easy to sleep, knowing that Eileen could pass on at any time. She survived the whole night, and was still sleeping when the new day's routines began. Occasionally her eyes would open, but there was no indication that she recognized anybody. The only visitors today, as expected, were Winston and Betty. We talked a lot together and even shared funny stories (such is our weird human resilience) while Eileen was in the midst of it, showing no reactions; but it was safe to assume that she appreciated the stories too. Soup and sandwiches were provided at lunchtime but only sandwiches in the evening. When the night staff came on duty they were surprised to find that Eileen was still with us.

We had both been very careful about our health. Most of the food we ate was organic, and we took regular exercise. Eileen was particularly concerned to avoid any kind of food that might promote cancer. If anyone should have lived a long and healthy life, it was Eileen. I had even contemplated celebrating our Golden Wedding at the age of 85. Yet, despite all these precautions, she had caught not one but two kinds of cancer at the same time. It seemed unfair. People who ate unhealthily often enjoyed robust health. Although Eileen's whole system was invaded by cancer, her heart was strong because of this healthy lifestyle. This was ironic: she was ready to go and be with the Lord, but her good health habits meant that the process was delayed.

So we came to the third night. It was during the night that Robert, the Downs Syndrome lad, came alive and played loud music. The nurses would turn down the volume, and he would immediately turn it up again. For him, it was a perfectly natural thing to do: it was all part of his holiday. When we saw him he would beam at us, quite unaware that he had done anything antisocial. We were glad that our door was so thick. During the daytime he would catch up on his sleep.

The next morning Eileen tried to speak. The only words we could identify were "Check the mobile". Chris and I had to go out while the nurses did things for Eileen. She vomited more bile while we were out and appeared to be in pain, as the 'driver' had not been working properly during the night.

As I washed, I was crying bitterly. All through these months, I had considered at each stage that things could not possibly get any worse, and time and again they had done so. It was hard for me to cling to my faith in God when there was so little evidence of his help and his presence. I knew that I would not always feel like this, but at the time it was like passing through a 'dark night of the soul'.

After breakfast I walked to the Mace store to top up my mobile. This gave me further opportunity for reflection. It would have been easy to pray, "Lord, let Eileen go quickly and peacefully and I will live a better life for you"; but that did not seem right. It left open the alternative to rebel against God if I was not conscious of his help. The right prayer was: "Lord, whatever happens, give me the ability to live a better life for you".

As Chris and I sat with Eileen, she was sleeping all the time. It was as if she was in some kind of limbo between death and resurrection. When Betty and Winston came, we again enjoyed plenty of talking, and hoped that Eileen was appreciating it. The staff continued to supply us with sandwiches, but I would be glad when I could eat a cooked meal again. At least, I would have no weight problem.

For the fourth night of our vigil, Eileen had a comfortable time. I slept for about three and a half hours and dozed at other times. When Eileen was breathing heavily, I had the satisfaction of knowing that she was alive; but when there was a change I would go over to the bed to check that she was still breathing. In the morning I derived comfort from Psalm 40, which assured me that God does hear my prayer.

There was some encouragement in the middle of the morning. Just after Winston and Betty arrived, Eileen opened her eyes and appeared to be responsive to what was happening around her. She tried to mouth some words. We heard her say 'cup of tea'. Deprived of food and drink for several days, she was obviously very thirsty. It would have been fitting if a deeply spiritual woman such as Eileen had mouthed some godly words at the close of her life, but this was not to be. The words were, however, appropriate. Northern Ireland has a strong 'coffee shop' culture, and we would visit these from time to time for little treats. Her sister Betty was an expert on the best ones to visit. Now, when we said something funny to Eileen, she smiled. It was as if we had got her back. Then it was time for the nurses to see to her needs. When this was done, she was sleeping deeply again. Angela, the nurse of whom Eileen had grown very fond, said that such an experience was very unusual. It was the Lord's good gift to us.

I remembered a very moving film called "Awakenings", in which a group of catatonic patients came alive for a while and behaved as normal people. It reminded me of the reality of the human spirit that survives all the limitations brought on by illness.

That evening Chris and I were given a cooked meal instead of the usual sandwiches. When Winston and Betty came back in the evening, they brought a cousin with them. We had a good talk round the bed, and again hoped that Eileen would feel included.

The fifth night was another one of cat-naps. We had not dreamed that our vigil would last so long. In the early morning I went to the Quiet Room for my devotions and played some Telemann as a background to my usual weeping and praying. I read from Psalm 130. God told me that he forgave me my sins and offered me hope. Even so, I could not understand why God was delaying taking Eileen when she was so ready to go and bringing me into this state of nervous exhaustion.

Gregor came on a visit and stayed for a short time. When he left I went for a short walk. I needed the fresh air. As I walked down a path, fringed by grass, it saddened me to think that Eileen would never again walk in such a place and watch the heads of grass blowing gently in the wind.

When I got back, the cleaner was in the room, and we had to stay out for a while. At last, we were able to return. Moments later Winston and Betty arrived. It was Chris who noticed, at that moment, that Eileen was no longer breathing. I tested, and found that was really so. We called a nurse, who confirmed it. The long period of slow release was over.

20
LARK ASCENDING

When my mother died just before midnight on the last day of 1996, it was an unexpectedly peaceful moment. When Eileen died, there was also a sense of peace, but I was at the same time pierced with agony as I reflected that the dividing line had been crossed and I would never again enjoy her companionship in this life.

I needed some time to weep at the bedside; but I was able to go out from there with strength for all the tasks that lay ahead. Chris and Winston went to the airport to collect Andrew. He therefore had opportunity to see his mother lying peacefully on her bed.

In all that had to be done, it was as if the Lord went ahead of us and made the decisions for us. With my two sons I went to Newtownards to register the death, and then on to the undertaker's to make arrangements for the funeral, which was to take place three days hence. As Eileen and I had discussed the arrangements together, it was a simple matter to state what was required. I even had a photograph with me that we could use for the programme. After we got home there was a welcome visit from the Bishop and his wife.

The music for the funeral had been chosen by Eileen. We would begin with Rutter's setting of the 23rd Psalm, which we had once sung in a concert in North Devon. The hymn 'Just as I am' was a reminder of Eileen's conversion so many decades ago. The hymns 'King of Kings, Majesty' and 'In Christ Alone' demonstrated her love of good, modern and biblical worship songs. It was only the closing music that was a subject for debate. Eileen had wanted some music composed by Andrew. As his equipment was not to hand, he was unable to compose anything new. There was a recording made about 9 years ago of Eileen singing an Irish folk song, 'Lark in the Clear Air' arranged by Andrew. He did not think it was professional enough, and we considered playing 'Gabriel's Oboe' instead; but in the end we decided to take the risk of playing the folk song. It turned out to be the right decision.

Nearly 200 people came to the funeral in Christ Church, Carrowdore I was glad that I had ordered 200 programmes. Our family stood at the door to welcome people in. This and all the other decisions seemed so right, and further evidence that God was guiding us all the way through. All three of us were given strength to speak. Andrew gave a short personal appreciation of his mother. Chris read a poem by Louis McNeice, who was buried in the same churchyard. I read out the eulogy that I had prepared so many months ago just in case of need. I had feared that I would break down, and had asked Kevin to be prepared to take over; but this was not necessary.

This is what I said:

"I speak of Eileen in the present tense, for I know that, in the Lord's presence, she is more fully alive than ever before. It has been an immense privilege to enjoy her companionship and her love during nearly 37 years of marriage. In this tribute I simply want to draw out some of the features of her life and character that I admire.

"First of all, she has a great love for the Lord. That is what dominates everything else. She was converted in late teens in Belfast through a visiting evangelist, and this led to her going to the Faith Mission Bible College in Edinburgh, working for a short time for that mission, and then, at the age of 24, going out via Singapore to Taiwan with OMF to work as a missionary. Shortly after our marriage she had a new experience of the Holy Spirit which made her very open to God's leading and brought her into a deeper experience of praise. All through our life together, I have derived much strength from her deep spirituality and her desire to see God honoured more and more. Even in her final illness, when considering how she should pray, she prayed for 'more of God'. I feel as if I have been married to a saint."

"Secondly, she has a great empathy with other people. Others find her very approachable. When she saw so many people around her with needs in our Wolverhampton days, she underwent counselling training so as to be able to help them. In her counselling ministry, as well as in informal friendships, she has been a good listener, and has imparted strength to others. Sometimes, when praying for others, she would even find some of the symptoms that they experienced present in her own body. People have told me how much their lives have been changed through contact with Eileen."

"Thirdly, she is deeply committed to family. Her home life at 306 Albertbridge Road was a very formative experience, and she has maintained a close relationship with her sister Betty. Our own relationship has been a very precious one, in which our love has grown deeper as we have grown older. She also has a deep love for our sons Andrew and Chris, and desires God's best for them."

"Fourthly, she has a great love for the natural world. Some of our best holidays have been when walking the South West Coast Path. It was love of the sea view from our window which drew us to Millisle to spend our days of retirement. We both came to enjoy the local bird life. Even when she was becoming unwell, she would sit in her chair, looking out of the window, and say, 'Isn't God good to give us this lovely view!'"

"Fifthly, she is a very creative person. On retirement, she set herself to acquire new skills. She took up upholstery and transformed my mother's old chairs. She tried her hand at painting, and two of her works now hang on our walls. She also took up patchwork and made a group of new friends through it."

"Sixthly, she is a woman of vision. Several local initiatives have come from her. It was through her that the Pharmacy Project first got under way, and those who attended the relaxation classes, at which she gave them foot massage, found it a good, healing experience. This year, in the second phase, a large group of enthusiastic women now attend the activities. Her vision for some land where disadvantaged young people could learn some agricultural skills, fired by a Monty Don initiative, has led to the creation of our Wildlife Garden. After attending a conference at St. Andrew's, Chorleywood, she had a vision of bringing the fire of God to the Ards Peninsula, and it seemed that the way to start was through a large praise gathering. Ministers began to meet regularly together, and out of that came Pentecost Praise. A further praise rally is planned for January."

"Seventhly. I see in her a wealth of goodness. She has certainly been an inspiration to me and gives me something to aim at after her death."

"Eighthly, she has a deep inner peace. When the cancer was first diagnosed this was certainly true, and it has continued. I am the one whose emotions have been so up and down. Naturally there have been negative feelings in the long time of waiting, as anyone would have, and physical problems can bring occasional despondency, but the peace has still been there most of the time, and people coming into her room have sensed it. She has not been ready to complain, even though life changed so suddenly for her. I know that she was ready for her promotion to heaven, and heaven is all the better for her presence."

"In short, she has been for me a constant companion, a wise adviser, an inspired visionary, a living example, a devoted lover and a best friend."

151

The Bishop preached well on Romans 8:29-30, with the Gospel in the forefront of his message. As we were about to leave the church, we listened to the recording of Eileen singing about the lark. That was the one part of the service in which my eyes filled with tears. It was moving, because it spoke of the freedom which Eileen now enjoyed, having been released from her body of sickness. People exclaimed, "We did not know she had such a good voice!"

The burial took place in the adjoining churchyard. As I watched the proceedings, I had the sober reflection that one day it would be my turn to be interred in that same place.

Time and again, people were to speak of that service as 'uplifting'. It was all that Eileen would have wished for. Through it we were able to witness to the power of the Resurrection and the joy of the Christian hope.

*

A few days later I went to the Christian Renewal Centre at Rostrevor to stay for a couple of days. Eileen and I had often enjoyed good fellowship there, and it seemed the right place to go for a time of quiet reflection. On this occasion I was not obliged to give a hand with the chores. While I was there I felt led to write a book about the experiences of the past year. Immediately I was given the title 'Lark Ascending'. It was my prayer right from the start that this book would help other people who, like Eileen and myself, had to face terminal illness.

*

At last I plucked up the courage to listen to the tape which Eileen had made for me. Her hesitancy and repetitiveness indicated that it had been a real struggle to prepare this, and I respected her for persevering with the task. It was very moving to sit there and listen to her voice once again.

What came out most clearly was the quality of our love for one another. How could I ever doubted that I would not have enough love to bring to the marriage?

She began: *"I thank God for the moment you came into my life and how we journeyed together along the path of healing and growing together as human*

152

beings and in our Christian walk. Thank you for the rock you have been and for the fun we've had together."

Looking to the future, she hoped I would continue to enjoy the house with its view, and that I would enjoy the walking holiday I had planned to take with the boys in the Spring. She looked back to the happy memories of bringing first Andrew and later Chris into the world. She said how proud she was to hear me preach the Gospel so clearly at an open air memorial service to Princess Diana on Paignton Green.

She said too how much she had enjoyed reading through the Journal. We had touched so many lives together. Underneath everything was the Rock of God's love and of our love for one another. She concluded: *"I hope the memory of that love will strengthen you in these difficult days.".*

*

Several days later, I was engaged in some sorting when I came across a book of Eileen's poems. Flipping through the pages, I came across a poem of hers which I do not think I had ever read. It was written on 3 March 2007. It provides a fitting conclusion and an unexpected verification of the title of this book:

> "At the place of tears
> There is the place of beauty.
> In the humbling of repentance
> We find the enfolding of His love.
> In the hard and lonely times
> We are drawn to His scarred feet.
> Then we hear the lark ascending,
> Sharing hope and the promise of spring."

If you wish to contact the author
email to rwed31@btinternet.com